Tears to Triumph

Tears to Triumph

Spiritual Healing for the Modern Plagues of Anxiety and Depression

MARIANNE WILLIAMSON

HarperOne

An Imprint of HarperCollins*Publishers*

HarperCollins books may be purchased for educational, business, or
sales promotional use. For information, please email the Special Markets Department
at SPsales@harpercollins.com.

FIRST HARPERCOLLINS PAPERBACK EDITION PUBLISHED IN 2017

Designed by Laura Lind Design

Library of Congress Cataloging-in-Publication Data is available upon request.

ISBN 978–0–06–220545–2

17 18 19 20 21   LSC(H)   10 9 8 7 6 5 4 3 2 1

In memory of Richard

Contents

Someday, emerging at last from the violent insight,

let me sing out jubilation and praise to assenting angels.

Let not even one of the clearly-struck hammers of my heart

fail to sound because of a slack, a doubtful,

or a broken string. Let my joyfully streaming face

make me more radiant; let my hidden weeping arise

and blossom. How dear you will be to me then, you nights

of anguish. Why didn't I kneel more deeply to accept you,

inconsolable sisters, and, surrendering, lose myself

in your loosened hair. How we squander our hours of pain.

How we gaze beyond them into the bitter duration

to see if they have an end. Though they are really

our winter-enduring foliage, our dark evergreen,

one season in our inner year—, not only a season

in time—, but are place and settlement, foundation and soil and home.

—From the Tenth Elegy, from
Rainer Maria Rilke's "Duino Elegies,"
translation by Stephen Mitchell

Preface

We all face times in our lives when the pain of existence seems too much to bear. For some of us, these experiences happen rarely, and when they do, the pain is relatively mild. But for others of us, excruciating pain can weigh us down and make the slightest comfort difficult to achieve. Deeper and deeper we fall into the well of our own tears, into a darkness that seems to have no bottom. We wonder where all this suffering comes from. And we wonder whether it will ever end.

If you, or someone you love, are living through one of those times—feeling that to take another breath, even to live another day, seems hard to contemplate—then I'm glad that you are reading this book. You may find here some pieces of the puzzle you have not yet explored. A mystery. Perhaps a miracle.

This doesn't mean that you won't have to make any effort. It doesn't mean that you won't have work to do on your own behalf. Miracles aren't a quick fix, or an easy answer. But they activate a spiritual power divinely authorized to help you. God is here, even here, in the midst of your suffering. And as you reach out to Him, He will reach back.

Consider the possibility now that anything could happen. I'm not asking you to believe this, but only to consider that it might be true. Simply thinking this thought—that miracles are possible—does more to pave the way for your healing than you can imagine. It opens the door to a realm of infinite possibilities, regardless of what you have been through or what you are going through now.

The pain you are going through is not what will determine your future; your future will be determined by who you are as you go through your pain. This is not to question the depth of your suffering. Within the mortal world, it is certainly real. But the reality in which you are ensnared is not itself what it appears to be, nor are you yourself quite the being you feel you are now. We can expand the definition of who you are, as well as what the world is—and your life will begin to change. Your human self might be in hell right now, but your divine self is literally untouched by your suffering. And your divine self is who you are.

Your subconscious mind is aware of your larger reality and will assume the role of showing it to you when you are ready for it to do so. This process will be one of the great journeys of your life, as you will see things you haven't seen and know things you haven't known. Your tears, your hopelessness, your fear, your anger, your guilt, your resentment, your remorse, your terror—none of these will be papered over or denied. You will not dissolve them by keeping them in the dark, but by exposing them to the light. And as you do, you will see beyond them such magnificence—in yourself and in the world—that you will actually bless the journey of your suffering, for it led you to yourself and to the meaning of your life. Spiritual healing doesn't lie in denying your pain, but in feeling it fully and surrendering it to God.

And then the miracles begin . . .

This book is a spiritual reflection on human suffering, both its cause and its transcendence. Spirituality is not some pale-pink, gauzy, psychologically unsophisticated understanding of the world. Rather, it represents the most profound elucidation of how the mind operates and how it filters our experience. It recognizes the extraordinary depth of our most fundamental yearning—our yearning for love—and the extraordinary pain that we feel when we don't find it.

There is an epidemic of depression in our world today, and a myriad of options for how to treat it. Just as there are natural remedies for disease within the body, there are natural remedies for disease within the mind. And by a "natural remedy" for depression I do not mean herbs or homeopathic remedies; I mean the practical application of love and forgiveness as a medicine for the soul.

As a society, we invite depression by trivializing love. We have sold our souls for a mess of pottage. Human existence is not just a random episode, with no higher purpose than that all of us should get what we want. Seen that way, with no overlay of spirit, our lives seem to have no ultimate meaning. And the soul craves meaning the way the body craves oxygen. In the absence of a spiritual framework, we know the mechanics of life but stop short of understanding it. Failing to understand life, we misuse it. And misusing it, we cause suffering—for ourselves and for others.

Every great religious and spiritual philosophy speaks to the issue of human suffering. This book only touches the surface of the spiritual depth of insight available in the great religious and spiritual teachings of the world, but hopefully it gets to a point often obscured behind veils of dogma and misunderstanding.

For instance: Buddha's spiritual journey began when he saw suffering for the first time; Moses was moved by the suffering of the Israelites; and Jesus suffered on the cross. But the point is not simply that Buddha saw suffering; the point is that he transcended it through his enlightenment. The point is not simply that the Israelites were enslaved; the point is that they were rescued and led to the Promised Land. The point is not simply that Jesus was crucified; the point is that he was resurrected. Human suffering was only the first part of an equation; what matters most is what happened after God showed *His* hand.

We too are suffering and observe suffering all around us; we too are enslaved by an internal pharaoh; and we too are dying on the cross of the world's cruelty and lack of reverence. Whether it occurred thousands of years ago or is occurring today, suffering is suffering, oppression is oppression, and cruelty is cruelty. These things are not ancient realities that don't exist anymore. They're not *gone.*

And neither is God's power to eradicate them. Spirit enlightened Buddha; Spirit delivered the Israelites; and Spirit resurrected Jesus. If we know our suffering is the same as theirs, it makes sense to seek a deeper understanding of their deliverance, that we might more easily invoke our own. How arrogant we are, and how blind, to think that our suffering is the same as it's always been, yet somehow we've improved on ways to deal with it. Are any of us under the impression that Buddha could have transcended suffering by making more money, getting a better job, or buying a better car? Or that the Israelites could have escaped slavery if they'd had another round of negotiations with Pharaoh or a private jet to take them to the Promised Land? Or that Jesus could have risen from the dead if only cryonics had been around then?

Humanity, over the past few hundred years, has lessened the incidence of some forms of suffering and increased the incidence of others. We've diminished the threat of polio, but increased the threat of nuclear disaster. We've diminished the dangers of travel, but increased the chances that our entire ecosystem will implode. And if we think we don't do "rape and pillage" anymore, take a look at what's going on around the world.

There is no worldly solution to the suffering, or self-destructiveness, of humanity today that can compare to the solutions offered by the great religions and spiritual philosophies of the world. Which is exactly why the ego mind has sought to co-opt them for its purposes. It has turned the power of peace into the power of the sword, both within the world and within our hearts.

Today's search for spiritual sustenance is not confined to a particular teaching. There is no right or wrong when it comes to Buddhism, or Judaism, or Christianity, or Islam, or Hinduism. They are all kaleidoscopic facets of one essential diamond. Whether we relate personally to the story of Buddha, Moses, Jesus, Mohammed, or Krishna; whether we understand truth more deeply when it is expressed by Carl Jung, Joseph Campbell, or *A Course in Miracles;* the essential themes at the heart of all these teachings are universal. They apply to all people, and most significantly, to all times.

The great religious figures and teachings of the world are God's gifts, a divine hand reaching down to touch the minds of those who are called to them. While the ego uses the outer aspects of these teachings to divide us—sometimes even as justification to destroy one another—their inner truths unite us by teaching us how to live with each other. On an internal level, the great religions of the world have always led to miracles. On an external level, they have as often led to violence and destruction. That must change, and will change, as more people come to recognize the mystical truths, the inner gold, that lie within them all. The greatest opportunity for humanity's survival in the twenty-first century lies not in widening our external horizons, but in deepening our internal ones. That applies to us personally, and it applies to us collectively.

And we will be sad until we do. Our bodies, our relationships, our careers, our politics, will continue to be sources of suffering when they should rather be sources of joy. Hidden within all great spiritual teachings is the key to turning that around. Once we find the key, and turn the key, we are amazed by what lies hidden behind the door that's been locked to God. We're not without hope; we just haven't been seeing it. We're not without power; we just haven't been claiming it. We're not without love; we just haven't been living it.

Seeing these things, our lives begin to change. Our minds are awakened. Miracles happen. And at last our hearts are glad.

ONE

Surrendering
Our Sorrow

All of us yearn for happiness and love, and sometimes we find it. Yet most of us are visited at some point by sorrow as well. A relationship, a job, a particular circumstance brought us happiness—but then something went wrong. At other times, we can't put our finger on why, but we feel no happiness and we feel no love.

Life, in fact, is not always easy, and dwelling gracefully within the space of deep sorrow can be very hard. Emotional torment, overwhelming grief, physical agony, screams from the very depths of our souls—why is such suffering a part of our experience? What does it mean? And how can we survive it and even transcend it?

A spiritual worldview does not skirt such questions; rather, it responds to them. In fact, these questions are at the heart of all great religious teachings, ranging from Buddha's first encounter with suffering when he left his father's royal compound, to the suffering of the Israelites when they were slaves under Pharaoh and when they wandered through the desert, to Jesus's suffering on the cross. The universal spiritual truths at the core of great religious teachings are a balm for the heart sent straight from the Mind of God.

Ironically, these truths are often more obscured than revealed by organized religion, concealing the extraordinary powers of comfort and inspiration they are meant to provide. This book seeks to reveal those principles, for they are coded messages pointing not only to the source of our suffering, but also to its healing.

Healing the heart is in fact God's specialty. Spirit reorders our thinking upon our request, in so doing bringing peace to our hearts. Inner peace does not emerge from an intellectual shift, but from a spiritual process that affects both body and soul. This shift is produced by a divine intercession that is far from metaphorical, as we align our thoughts with those of God.

Theology alone does not bring comfort. But spiritual principles, when practically applied, are gateways to inner peace. This book is about turning these principles into an alchemical brew of personal transformation, using the insights of great religious truths to assuage the pain that is a part of being human.

Simply waking up in the morning and going through the daily routines of a normal existence can be emotionally or even physically burdensome. Excruciating pain can weigh upon the heart for months or even years, obliterating all joy and making the slightest comforts impossible. Traumatic memories can cut the psyche like razors. Suffering can overwhelm all else, and even if we think there is a God, He can seem at such moments like He is very far away.

But God is never far away, because God is in our minds. We are free to think whatever we wish to think. The door to emotional deliverance is primarily a mental one. By aligning our thoughts with His thoughts, we can awaken to Him in the midst of our suffering. We can find Him in the midst of our darkness. And we can walk with Him into the light that lies beyond. The universe is wired for God's light the way a house is wired for electricity, and every mind is like a lamp. But a lamp must be plugged in for it to shed any light. With every prayer, we plug in to the light. With every realization of our mistakes and willingness to atone for them, we plug in to the light. With every apology we give and receive, we plug in to the light. With every act of forgiveness, we plug in to the light. With every five minutes of meditation, we plug in to the light. With every thought of mercy, we plug in to the light. With every moment of faith, we plug in to the light.

The search for God is a search for light, and outside that light we are sorrowful indeed. Within it, we are healed and made whole.

FALLING INTO A
DEEP, DARK VALLEY

I know something about suffering, as twice I've been diagnosed as clinically depressed. I've also experienced personal tragedy and the deaths of loved ones. I've suffered through devastating betrayals and disappointments. I've felt on more than one occasion that I had lost any chance of happiness I might have ever had. I've been up close and personal with suffering, not only in my own life, but also in the lives of many others in the course of my career. Nothing gives you x-ray vision into the suffering of others like having suffered yourself. I know the face of depression and I know it well.

As someone who has always viewed things through a mystical lens—even before I really understood what that meant—I've always seen events in my life in the context of a spiritual journey. I've viewed painful times in my life as part of a mysterious unfolding, as dark nights of my soul for which, no matter how devastating, I needed to be fully present. However deep my suffering, I didn't want to be anesthetized as I went through it. Like an expectant mother who wants to give birth naturally, rejecting drugs during labor because she wants to experience "natural childbirth," I wanted to be fully available to the depths of my pain. Why? Because I knew it had something to teach me. I knew that somehow, in some way, my suffering would lead to a blazing new dawn in my life—but only if I was willing to endure the deep, dark night preceding it.

None of this is to romanticize suffering. Sleepless nights, obsessive thoughts, extreme mental and emotional pain are nothing to view lightly. But my journeys through deep sadness have ultimately shown me as much about light as they have about darkness—for in coming to understand my suffering, I've come to understand myself more deeply. On the other side of my suffering, I've seen things that I wouldn't have seen otherwise. I've seen ways I have contributed to my own disasters. I've seen that love isn't a game and that it should be taken seriously. I've seen that other people's feelings are as important as my own. I've seen that external things are not what matter. I've seen that life lived with any purpose but love is a life that will lead to sorrow. I've seen that love is more powerful than evil. I've seen that nothing but the love of God can be guaranteed. And I've seen that life does indeed go on.

Regret, remorse, humiliation, physical pain, grief, failure, loss—all of these can be excruciating. Yet as difficult as they can be to endure, they can also pave the way at times to illumination: conscience, forgiveness, humility, contrition, appreciation, gratitude, and faith. Sometimes we end up looking back on times of deep emotional pain as having been the crucibles out of which emerged the truth of who we are.

I've learned a lot from the midnight blues, as agonizing as they can be. It is often during sleepless nights that we come face-to-face with monsters too easily shooed away during daylight hours, carrying with them not only sorrow but information. That which is difficult is not always that which is bad. We might see something that needs to change within us, what we need to atone for, how our character defects or neurotic patterns are ruining our lives, what trespasses we need to forgive, and what amends we need to make. We might at last come clean with God, asking His help in forgiving ourselves, and then realize His mercy as we pray for another chance to get things right. We might grieve loved ones we lost, and finally come to feel the eternal bond that keeps us one with them forever. On such nights we often cry tears that we simply need to cry.

At times the light *derives* from realizations that we come to while we are in the darkness. Periods of suffering are not always detours on the journey to enlightenment but can serve as significant stops along the way. Personal demons that emerge from the dark cave of deep sadness cannot just be "treated"; they must be dissolved through the light of self-awareness. Everything that needs to be looked at must be looked at; everything that needs to be understood must be understood; and every prayer that needs to be prayed must be prayed.

And this can take time. A period of emotional suffering is often not simply a *symptom* of our depression as much as a necessary factor in healing it. It can be what we need to move through, and best not avoid, in journeying to the place where we suffer no more.

Sometimes, therefore, we have to make room for our emotional pain. Months of grief might be at times what we need to go through, processing the mysteries of love and loss in order to finally see that in spirit there is no loss and that in God there is always hope. Such mourning is a sacred journey, and it cannot and should not be rushed. If we have forty-five tears to cry, then crying seventeen is not enough. Deep sorrow is a fever of the soul, and within the psyche as within the body, the fever breaks when the fever breaks. The tendency to repair—an inborn immune system always moving in the direction of healing—exists in the mind as well as in the body. We simply need to give it time.

The potential for heartbreak always exists; it is part of the human experience. Where there is love, there is happiness. But where the bonds of love are broken, there is pain. Given the fact that the world is so dominated by fear, and so resistant in many ways to love, how could our hearts not be torn at times by the pain of simply living here?

And once you've lived enough, you know this. You come to live with it, and to live with it gracefully. You learn to take the hits, and to know that they're simply part of living. "Hello darkness, my old friend; I've come to talk with you again" is more than a song lyric by Simon and Garfunkel; it describes an attitude of acceptance that this week, or this month, or even this year might be hard—but you know you will live through it. And in some ways, who we become *because* we lived through it is someone more alive—perhaps even more beautiful— than who we were before. In the words of Elisabeth Kübler-Ross, "Should you shield the canyons from the windstorms you would never see the true beauty of their carvings."

Depression is an emotional fall, sometimes into a very deep, dark valley. That is true. Yet a life of spiritual triumph is not one in which we never fall into that valley; it is one in which, if and when we do fall, we've learned how to get ourselves out of it. We need emotional muscles in order to rise up emotionally, just as we need physical muscles in order to rise up physically. And developing those muscles is the work of the soul. It is the search for God and the finding of our true selves.

God is not outside us but within—the Love that is the essence of who we truly are. We live within God and God lives within us. The pain of the world is the unbearable suffering of living outside the circle of our relationship to God, for outside that relationship we are separate from ourselves. What could be more depressing than to live in separation from who we are? And what could be more natural than the fact that we seek wholeness in places where our hearts have been torn? Falling to our knees in pain has been, for many of us, how we first fell to our knees in prayer. At moments when the pain is simply too much to take, the body itself is wired for humility before God.

No matter what problem has entered our lives, no matter what pain has seared our hearts, the one fundamental answer is the attainment of the peace of God. *A Course in Miracles* teaches that we think we have many different problems, but we only really have one: our separation from God. This book is about the alleviation of our suffering: sometimes through prayer, sometimes through forgiveness, and always through the surrender and release of all our thoughts that are not of God.

Therein lies inner peace.

CHANGING OUR MENTAL FILTERS

Surrendering thoughts that are not of God means surrendering thoughts that are not of love. Each of us has a spiritual immune system—a system that exists to heal the injured psyche just as the physical immune system heals the physical body—but it takes conscious effort to activate its power. It's not always easy to surrender our lovelessness, especially when we're in emotional pain. Yet in order to heal, we must. Spiritual healing is *work* in the sense that it isn't passive, but active. It is a medicine we co-create with God.

This medicine is a miracle. It is a shift from primary identification with the suffering self to identification with the spiritual self. This mental illumination lights the fire of God within us, a fire that will burn in time through every thought that causes us pain. It guides us to a reinterpretation of everything that has occurred in our lives, replacing a mental filter that ensures our pain with a mental filter than ensures our deliverance from pain. It does this by guiding us into the radicalism of forgiveness and love.

Miracles are thoughts, and thoughts produce everything. Thought is the level of cause; the world as we know it is the level of effect. A miracle is a shift in perception from fear to love, changing an effect in our lives by changing the thinking that caused it.

Most of our suffering is due less to our circumstances than to our thoughts about them. In fact, the world is merely a projection of our thoughts. Everything we go through is filtered through either the mind of love or the mind of fear; love creates peace, and fear creates pain. Fear is not a thing in and of itself; rather, it is the absence of love. Since the thought system that dominates the world is one that repudiates love, it is a prison in which we are bound to suffer. The only way to escape our suffering is to rise above the thought system that creates it.

The pain we experience while living in this world should not be denied, of course, but it can be transcended. Miracle-minded thinking does not suppress our emotions; rather, it brings them up so we can place them on a path to true healing.

Healing occurs when we identify our painful feelings and then place them in His hands, praying that the thoughts which produced the feelings will be realigned with His. Releasing a situation to God means releasing our *thoughts* about it, that they might be changed on a causal level. That which is placed on the altar is then altered.

It would be a violation of our free will for God to rearrange our thoughts without our consciously having asked Him to do so, but once we ask, our prayers are answered. Our suffering having been surrendered, an alchemical healing process begins immediately. Situations are miraculously transformed as our thoughts are divinely shifted.

Where we've been holding on to bitterness, we are guided to the ways of forgiveness. Where we've been holding on to the past, we're gently shown new possibilities in the present. Where our general outlook has been negative, we begin to see things through a more positive lens. The point is that once we are *willing* to see things differently—to conspire with a God who, in the words of *A Course in Miracles,* "outwits our self-hatred"—then the healing begins.

Your consciousness is illumined, at first perhaps just slightly, but the tiny crack of light you allowed into your mind will expand into a miraculous blaze. A softening in a relationship will become inevitable; every book that would help you falls at your feet; a friend who might have helpful insight just happens to call. Realizations about how your own behavior might have been different start to occur to you.

A spiritual perspective does not deny your pain, or any aspect of your human experience. It simply denies its power over you. It gives you the strength to endure when the tears are falling, and the power to invoke miracles that lie beyond.

FROM ILLUSIONS TO TRUTH

A miracle changes how we view the world, piercing the veil of illusion that keeps us trapped in pain and suffering. A prayer for a miracle is not a request that a situation *be* different, but a request that we *see* it differently. Only when our thoughts are changed will the effects of our thoughts be changed as well. Only when we see beyond the illusions of the world will we be lifted above the sorrow they produce. And what are these illusions? They are the manifestations produced by fear that would hide the face of love.

The material world is a vast matrix of illusion created by the mortal mind. The point of spiritual seeking is not just to realize that the world is filled with illusions, however; it is also to realize the ultimate truth that lies beyond them. To say that the world as we know it is not our ultimate reality is not to say we do not *have* an ultimate reality. We *do* have an ultimate reality—which lies beyond our bodies, beyond our mistakes, and beyond this world at all.

We are not small specks of dust—simply short-lived, finite, imperfect mortal beings with no greater purpose than to grasp pathetically for some happiness before we inevitably suffer and die. And while we hold ourselves hostage to such an insane perception of what it means to be human, we are doomed to mental and emotional anguish. Instead, we can embrace a deeper truth: that we are spirits, not just bodies. That we are great and glorious beings on this earth with great and glorious missions, and having forgotten this, we have been cast into an outer kingdom of pain and despair. Our task, then, is to find a way back to this nobler vision of who we really are, that the pain of our forgetfulness might cease.

Our existential pain results from living within a hallucinatory experience and thinking it is real. The three-dimensional plane of experience is very real to our mortal selves, but something deep within us knows that there is something more. This doesn't mean that you didn't suffer through this or that human experience; but it does mean that the "you" who suffered through it isn't the real you. As our thoughts are rearranged regarding who we are in *relation* to the experience, our experience of the experience transforms. This doesn't invalidate our mortal suffering, but it validates our capacity to rise above it. The real "you" is love, unaffected by that which is not love. Your spirit—God's creation that is your ultimate reality—is unalterable and unaffected by the lovelessness of the world.

The human mind is basically split. Just as part of the mind knows who we are, and sees clearly beyond the worldly veil of illusion, part of the mind is delusional and blind. Learning to dismantle the delusional mind, the fear-based ego, is the path of enlightenment. Just as darkness is cast out by light, fear is cast out by love. The ego is ultimately dissolved and replaced by the mind of spirit, which is love.

Love is the Truth as God created us; when our thoughts are not loving, we are literally *not being ourselves.* Psychically, every loveless thought is an act of self-annihilation. A world that neither recognizes the primacy of love nor fosters its expression is a depressing world indeed.

Enlightenment, which is infinite compassion, is the only true antidote to our suffering. This cure does not necessarily happen quickly, or without deep and even gut-wrenching work. For the world can be hard, and our resistance to love can be very strong. But our willingness is everything, and God responds fully to our slightest invitation that He help us see things differently. A spiritual reinterpretation of events gives us miraculous authority—to command the winds, to part the waters, and to break all chains that bind us. The power of God cannot and will not fail. We begin to feel peace where before we knew agonizing anxiety, to feel hope where before we saw no possibility of breakthrough, and to learn to forgive and to feel forgiven.

Seeing our lives through a spiritual lens is not a less sophisticated but a more sophisticated way of interpreting our experience. The love that saves us is not an abstraction or a gooey, wimpy sentimentality. Compassion is the greatest power in the universe. The mind that minimizes the power of love to release us from our suffering is the mind that creates our suffering to begin with, and then vigilantly maintains it.

The loveless mind is the ultimate cause behind every disaster and every tear. The only thing to be saved from, really, is the insane thinking that dominates this planet. Aligning with the divine self, then, is our salvation. For we suffer to the extent that we identify with the brokenness of the world, and our power to heal lies in knowing that we actually are not *of* this world. Because we are children of God, we need not suffer the world's insanity as we do.

Expanding our thinking beyond the confines of three-dimensional reality, we free ourselves of those confines. We forge new pathways in our brains, and in our experiences. We avail ourselves of quantum possibilities that otherwise would not appear.

This process is not an instantaneous "Eureka!" moment. A depressed person doesn't just say "Oh I get it now" and then quickly move on. It isn't easy, for instance, to forgive someone who did, in fact, betray us; to remain optimistic that the future can be better when the past has been tragic; to embrace the possibility of an eternal connection with someone whose abandonment or death has devastated us. But when we are *willing*, with the help of God, to see what we do not see now, then our inner eye is opened. We extend our perceptions beyond the veil of worldly illusion and are delivered to a world beyond.

None of this is easy, for our prison walls are thick. They're fortified by the appearances of the material world and by the mental agreements of our species. Humanity has been dominated by a fear-based thought system for ages, and enlightenment is a radical repudiation of the basic tenets of that worldview. Few things are more revolutionary than finding true happiness in a suffering world.

WISDOM

Enlightenment involves a retraining of our mental muscles as we go against the emotional and psychological gravity of the fear-based mind.

The ego seeks to preserve itself by luring us into loveless thoughts at every opportunity. And make no mistake about it; it seeks not merely to annoy us, but to make us suffer greatly: not merely to inconvenience us, but if at all possible to kill us. From addiction to warfare, the ego seeks not merely to withhold love, but to destroy it.

Fear gives rise to a variety of negative emotions, some of them relatively harmless and some genuinely insane. One confluence of fear-based emotions is commonly called depression. Depression is an implosion of negativity that suppresses, at least temporarily, our ability to "just get over it." It is like an emotional muscle spasm in which we are unable to move out of a fixed and painful place.

Given the state of the world today—given the fear and destruction all around us—depression among any of us is understandable. Life on earth can indeed be heartbreaking. But deep sadness, even intense emotional suffering, need not break us. It is part of the human experience, part of our spiritual journey. Even the happiest life can have deeply sad days. Once we accept this fact, making space for it in our consciousness, we stop seeing every bout of depression as an intruder that has to be shooed out of the house immediately.

The fact that we can *be* heartbroken is part of our deep humanity; it is not a weakness in our character. A weakness, if anything, is our fear of looking at our suffering more authentically and our resistance to dealing with it more wisely.

The wisest question when we are deeply sad is not, "How can I end or numb this pain immediately?" The wisest question is, "What is the meaning of this pain?" or, "What does it reveal to me? What is it calling me to understand?"

An honest inquiry into the spiritual significance of our pain does not prolong it, but rather hastens its end. Whether we grow from our suffering or succumb to it lies primarily in whether we succeed in finding a spiritual lesson in even the most excruciating circumstances. Searching for those lessons is the search for wisdom, and the search for wisdom is the search for peace. In the words of the philosopher Friedrich Nietzsche, "To live is to suffer, to survive is to find some meaning in the suffering."

In today's world, the search for wisdom is trivialized and often undervalued. Yet while reason can analyze a situation, only wisdom can deeply understand it. The search for wisdom is not some philosophical amusement without practical applicability. The search for wisdom is a search for how to live our lives more responsibly, both as individuals and as a species. Without wisdom, we often make terrible decisions. We become emotionally unsteady, routinely plunging headfirst into self-destructive situations. And then, though we're forced to spend huge amounts of time and energy trying to fix situations caused by our lack of wisdom, we spend comparatively little time on learning how to live more wisely in the future.

That's why learning what our pain has to teach us is so important: so that on the other side of it, we're less likely to experience the same pain again. The mind that led us into hell to begin with is always more than glad to welcome us back.

How odd that we spend so much time treating the darkness and so little time seeking the light. The ego loves to glorify itself by self-analysis, yet we do not get rid of darkness by hitting it with a baseball bat. We only get rid of darkness by turning on the light.

In searching for God, we do enter the darkness but only in order to expose it to the light. Like Isis roaming the countryside to reassemble the scattered pieces of her beloved Osiris, we must retrieve the unintegrated pieces of our self. And from that act of love, we bear new life. When we emerge from times of deep sorrow and pain, something much more significant occurs than our simply becoming happy again. Having glimpsed the deepest darkness, we start to see the light of God more clearly. Truly, if God is anywhere, He is with us on our darkest days. And when our darkest days are no longer with us, we do not forget that He was with us when they were.

Your torment during this process is not just a cold and clinical occurrence, but a holy process leading not only to the end of your pain, but to the beginning of a new sense of self. You will suffer, perhaps, but in time you will heal. A new chapter of your life will emerge from the ashes. As it says in Revelation 21:4 and also in *A Course in Miracles,* "God Himself will wipe away all tears."

Our civilization has an immature and neurotic obsession with always trying to be happy. And yet sometimes it is through having cried our tears that we can see at last our blessings. In the words of Ernest Hemingway, "The world breaks everyone, and afterward, many are strong at the broken places." The real question, for anyone who suffers, is whether we want to be one of those who are strengthened by the experience.

It's a psychological art form, mastering the balance between permitting ourselves to honor our suffering and making a simultaneous commitment to surviving the experience. To say, "I know this is a terrible time. But it is not without meaning, and I am committed to finding out what that meaning is. I am committed to opening myself to the lessons to be learned here." And the lesson is always, in some way, the expansion of our capacity to love.

There is only one real problem in life: that someone turned their back on love. Yet no matter how intense the ego's demonic hold on the mind—from mild annoyance to outright evil—God's love is so great, and His mercy so infinite, that He will always have the final say. The universe is always ready to start again, to send another opportunity for love in a never-ending wave of "Try this, then." The universe of love is incapable of exhaustion. It is always creating new possibilities, new varieties of miraculous opportunities. There is nothing that we could ever do or that could ever happen to us—nothing, no matter how sinister—that can ultimately prevail against the Will of God. Knowing this is the dawn of understanding. Believing it is the beginning of faith. Experiencing it is the miracle of new life.

This mindset lifts even a painful experience to a higher emotional frequency, creating a sense that angels are holding us even while we cry. In the words of the Greek playwright Aeschylus, "He who learns must suffer, and, even in our sleep, pain that cannot forget falls drop by drop upon the heart, and in our own despair, against our will, comes wisdom to us by the awful grace of God."

TWO

Through the Darkness into the Light

Jonathan was wearing an expensive dark suit, a crisp white shirt, and a beautiful necktie when he walked into my apartment. I could tell he didn't exactly know who he was coming to see or whether he thought he should even be here. A psychiatrist friend had asked if we could visit.

He couldn't resist getting in some patronizing jabs about what he saw as my lack of credentials, making sure I knew he was too smart to see someone like myself under normal circumstances. But I silently surrendered my judgment of what I felt was an awfully smug attitude. Sitting down, I simply looked him in the eye and asked, "So why are you here, Jonathan?"

"Oh," he said with an artificial glibness. "Daniel just thought it might be a good idea for us to kick around a few ideas about some things I've been going through."

"Really?" I asked. Knowing Daniel, I felt it was highly unlikely he'd suggested that Jonathan come to me for a session so we could "kick around a few ideas." I held his gaze.

There was silence for a few seconds before he finally said, very quietly, "No, not really."

Then, looking as though he was in pain, his entire body went limp. He looked away from me and whispered the words, "I've lost everything."

I put a box of Kleenex on the table in front of him. I remained very quiet, wanting to meet him at the depth of his sorrow.

Then I asked him gently, "Can you tell me what happened?"

And he began to talk.

Jonathan's story, though deeply painful to him, was somewhat familiar in the annals of modern suffering. He'd had a beautiful wife, a large home, a large legal practice, and a large life—until the large bills got too much for him, and he made some desperate moves—not all of them legal. Ultimately, he lost his wife, lost his money, lost his home, lost his license to practice law, and just barely escaped prison. He was living now with his sister and her family, trying desperately to recover his sense of self-worth and find hope for a new beginning. Understandably, he was deeply depressed.

With tears in his eyes, he continued: "I did know better. It's not like I'm just an asshole and didn't care about what I was doing. I was just . . . I kinda . . . things sort of got away from me." He laughed sardonically.

I waited a beat. "Were drugs or alcohol involved?" I asked.

"No," he said. "But they might as well have been. I feel like I was high on something."

"Yeah, well, you were sort of high on a certain kind of life," I said.

"Yes, I was," he said. He sighed, "Yes, I was."

"So let me see," I said slowly. "You used to be a big *macher* and now you're not. The wife you thought would love you through thick and thin left you once things got too thin. You lost your way of making a living; you don't have the money to pay rent; and you're living at a relative's house. Have I got this right?"

"Yeah," he said, as he reached for a Kleenex. His facial muscles were starting to relax now. The truth was out. The pretense was over.

"So in other words, there's nothing more to lose. There's no façade to hold up. You can finally relax, because you've fallen all the way down."

Silence.

"Does any little part of you feel relieved?" I asked.

He didn't know where I was going, but I could tell I had struck a chord. He smiled ruefully.

"In a certain way, weirdly, yeah . . ."

"You know, sometimes it's when things are this terrible that they start to get better," I said. "Your entire life is broken, I understand that. But are you open to the possibility that anything good could come from this?"

"Well, I know that they can't be worse. And I'm here. So obviously I'm looking for some hope."

"There's a Zen Buddhist saying about emptying your cup so it can be filled," I told him. "Sometimes the best thing that can happen is that our lives become empty, so they can be filled again with something better. I think that on a subconscious level, you emptied your cup."

A year earlier, Jonathan wouldn't have heard a word I was saying. But where he was in his life at that moment, he was open in a way he would not have been before. He was seeking help, and he'd developed some humility before someone who might be able to provide some.

Having lost everything that the world had to offer (or so he thought), Jonathan could now hear some ideas that didn't fit his normal thought patterns. Sometimes it's when we feel that all hope is lost that a better life begins to emerge. Our hearts crack open, and then our minds crack open. It's when the ego says, "It's all over," that God says, "Now we can begin."

"Your pride has been destroyed by all this, right?" I asked.

"That's for sure," he said.

"But is pride a good thing?" I asked him softly. Emotionally, he was like a burn victim, and I wanted my words to be a salve, not an agitant.

"I want to ask you a question, Jonathan. Was that life you were living really working for you?" I waited. "Because you destroyed it yourself, you know," I continued. "None of that stuff happened out of nowhere. You subconsciously ripped apart your own life. Do you know why you did that?"

He thought for a moment. "No," he said quietly. "I was obviously crazy."

"Maybe you were," I said. "You were definitely crazy to self-sabotage, but on another level you weren't crazy at all to blow it all up.

"The life you had created was unsustainable. It was a tall tree with very shallow roots. The universe always destroys what is ultimately unsound, but it doesn't destroy *you*, Jonathan. In fact, all those things were coming down around you so that the real you could rise up!

"Even our mistakes can lead us to a better place, once we surrender to what we obviously hadn't been surrendered to before. The issue is to become now who you weren't before so you can start again from a different place. Is there any way that you're a better person for having gone through all this?"

He looked as though to a far horizon, but said nothing.

"Look," I said. "There is a lot to deconstruct here. You're going to have to look at issues that your entire life was set up to help you avoid. Like, why you married someone who was only in it for the money. And I'm sorry, but on some level you knew. And why you wanted to live such a grandiose life to begin with when you knew it was more than you could handle. And why you were willing to break the law when you knew not only that it was wrong, but also that it could bring the entire house down. A lot of self-hatred was bound up in all that behavior, you know. If you want to heal and start over, you're going to have to look at all this, Jonathan. And it will feel horrible at times. It will feel like you are sticking needles in your eyes. But your willingness to do it, to face what really happened here—to atone for your mistakes and forgive everyone else for theirs—is everything."

I waited a few seconds. "There's bad news here, but there's good news, too," I said slowly. "The bad news is, you lost everything. But the good news is, you're down to your true, authentic, heartbroken self now. I know you're humiliated and you hate yourself and you're frightened at the moment, but be very clear: you set this up because on some level you wanted it to happen. You wanted that entire ridiculous lifestyle to crash, because you knew on some level it was bull. You turned a lot of things into idols, and idols always fall. You wanted to get caught because you knew on some level you deserved to. And you wanted to lose everything because you knew on some level it was the only way you would humble yourself enough to ever know anything that was real or important."

He nodded slowly.

To Jonathan right then it seemed like the worst thing that could have happened, had happened. But he would slowly see that this could also be the best thing. Most importantly, that it was an inevitable thing; for a house comes down when its foundation is rotten. Recognizing that, he could rebuild his life from a new foundation. Yes, he had a lot of reconciling to do, beginning with himself. He had a lot of atoning to do, and a lot of shadows he needed to face. The process would not be fun. But it was also true that he was getting his first glimpses of the spiritual journey, discovering a path that would take him out of his current darkness. Using this experience to mine the inner gold of self-awareness, he would learn to realign his thinking, forgive himself and others, and rise to a better place than he had ever been.

"Your mistakes don't make you less lovable, Jonathan. I know you feel like you are unlovable, but you're not. People make mistakes; you just happened to make a whole lot of them at one time!

"You might not believe me when I say this, but a time will come when you will value some things you never valued before, and you won't even care that much what it took to get you there."

"I already do, in a way," he said. "I never thought I'd be so grateful for things. My four-year-old niece came into my room this morning with pancakes she said she made for me, and I started crying."

"That doesn't mean you're insane, you know. It means you're finally getting sane enough to know what's really important. I know it's a terrible ego bruise that you lost so much. I know you're depressed and shattered right now. It happens.

"But welcome to the club, Jonathan. You and I and pretty much everyone at some point have swerved from who we really are and then crashed against a wall. It doesn't mean we're any worse than anyone else. It just means that personal power is a sad thing to mismanage. You had to have been very powerful to mess things up so badly, don't you think?"

He had a faint smile on his face now.

"When I was a little girl, my father used to say, 'Proud days soon pass.' You were a bit of a golden prince, Jonathan, and you got struck down because it had to happen. For all your talent and all your intelligence, the universe had to show you who's God. This was all just one huge initiation, actually. And now you will become a king—inside, for real."

Jonathan laughed. A big, hearty laugh. He was quiet for a few moments and then said, "I was such a jerk."

"So this is a surprise to you?" And I laughed too. "But all of us are jerks at times, Jonathan. It's going to make you more merciful to others when you see all the mercy God's going to show you.

"The point here isn't that your career will come back, though if you work for it, then of course it will. The point isn't that you'll get back on your feet financially, though in time I know you will. The point isn't that you will love again, though you know as well as I do that of course you will. Yet none of those things will represent your triumph. Your triumph will lie in understanding that there is no reason to do anything, or even to live at all, except to become the man you're capable of being. Once you see this—this blazing light of spiritual realization that all of us are bound to see in time—then everything else will follow. You'll fall to your knees and then rise to new heights. All the good things will come back again, but this time they'll be built on a solid foundation, and this time they will stay."

Our session that day didn't take away all of Jonathan's sadness, but it helped start him on a new journey. He knew he would have to go through this dark night of the soul and learn from it; it wouldn't be easy, but he was prepared to begin. There would be books for him to read, spiritual paths for him to discover, and most importantly, insights and epiphanies about himself and his life that he would not be privy to unless he did the deep inner digging necessary.

Not everything he needed to think about would be fun to remember, and some of it would clearly be awful. But such memories, should he meet them with genuine atonement and humility before God, would turn into diamonds that would illumine his life if he allowed them to.

We were silent for a couple of minutes, and I asked him whether he'd like to say a prayer.

"Yes, please."

And we did.

Dear God,

I surrender to You

The pain that is in my heart.

I give to you my failure,

My shame,

My loss,

My devastation.

I know that in You, dear God,

All darkness is turned into light.

Pour forth Your Spirit

Upon my mind,

And help me to forgive my past.

Make my life begin again.

Restore my soul

And bring me peace.

Comfort me in this painful hour,

That I might see again

My innocence and good.

I have fallen, dear God,

And I feel I cannot rise.

Please lift me up and give me strength.

Set my feet upon the path to peace

And help me not to stray again.

I pray for forgiveness.

I am crushed by my failure.

Please show me who I am to You,

That self-hate shall not defeat me.

Help me remember and reclaim my good.

Help me become

Who You would have me be,

And live the life you would have me live,

That my tears shall be no more.

Amen

When we ended the prayer, he wiped tears from his eyes.

As we walked to the door, I saw a lightness in his gait that hadn't been there when he arrived. The last thing he said to me that day was "Thank you." It seemed to come from a very tender place.

EATING THORNS

In order to create their beautiful plumage, peacocks sometimes eat thorns. Hard, pointed, razorlike objects are processed in their abdomens and then contribute to feathers with colors and shapes unmatched throughout nature for their extraordinary beauty. So it is with us.

Often, that which is the hardest to digest, to process, to integrate into our life experiences is what ultimately transforms us in a positive way. We become who we are meant to be sometimes by having to eat some hard-edged, bitter thorns of human experience. Jonathan is not all that different from all of us. Who among us hasn't stumbled?

We failed at relationships, and then those failures propelled us to more deeply understand what relationships are for and how to master the art of loving. We grieved the loss of a loved one and then came through the experience more appreciative of every day we have with those we love. We lost at business and then looked back at the loss as the business education we obviously needed. We were betrayed and then experienced the incredible power of forgiveness. We made mistakes and then experienced God's mercy as we acknowledged, atoned for, and made amends for them all. Anything and everything can be a platform for a miracle.

Sometimes it is our suffering that mysteriously delivers us to the holiness within ourselves. Having tasted that which is most bitter, we often taste that which is most sweet. Our hearts having been broken, they then can break open. The tiny light of hope that we glimpse in the midst of our suffering can become a light so bright that the immensity of its power seems second only to the depth of its tenderness. Having entered the regions of our personal hopelessness, we find at last where true hope lies. We come to understand more clearly who we are and why we are on the earth. The light that can lead us out of suffering leads us into the arms of God.

The most depressed periods of life can be initiations into our spiritual power, as we come to take an honest look at the deeper forces at play in our personal dramas.

Such is the spiritual path, and it is indeed a hero's journey. The hero's name might be Jonathan, or something else—it is your name and my name and everyone's name. It is the journey away from the ego's destructiveness, as we rise, however bloodied from the climb, to the emotional peak of nakedness before God, there to drop our masks and embrace our true selves. Of course it is painful to endure the death throes of the false self, that self-sabotaging enemy who, if allowed to, runs rampant through every corner of our lives. But as false parts of our personalities begin to die, the truth of who we are gets a chance at last to breathe. Every thought of fear, every behavioral pattern that is based on fear, and every mask we wear that is filled with fear is hiding a light so bright within us that its gorgeousness exceeds the beauty of any beauty in the world.

And that is the ultimate deliverance from suffering—the realization that we can be better people because of it. The spiritual journey from emotional pain to inner peace entails a transformation of our personalities, from being someone weakened by suffering to someone honed by it. Yes, we must look at the darkness within ourselves, and forgive others for the darkness that we see within them, in order to experience the miracle of love that only forgiveness brings. Yet in so doing we emerge victorious. We reintegrate the dissociated pieces of personality that lay submerged within the dark caves of fear into which they had been cast by the ego mind. Slowly, perhaps, but surely, we are led by God to emerge at last into the light of our true selves.

And within that light, endless miracles abound. For miracles occur naturally as expressions of love. We grow less imprisoned by our fears as we release them to thoughts of love. No longer in denial about our issues, we atone and learn to forgive ourselves. No longer blaming others, we are able to forgive them. We experience a childlike surrender into the arms of God, an experience of cosmic re-parenting from which we grow at last into the adults we were meant to be. The ego would have us cower in a state of endless infantilization and victimhood. God would have us stand up tall, the mantle of grace and power and victory around us. This is the greatest story, the story of all stories, and it is the story of every one of us.

THREE

The Case Against Numbness

The lovely young woman who sat before me seemed bewildered, but she was looking for answers. Miranda had been diagnosed with a depressive disorder and was taking several medications simultaneously. I asked her whether she would share a bit of her story so I could understand why.

In listening to her, I heard of a journey much like that of many young people in their twenties doing the admittedly difficult work of trying to figure out who they are. While I wouldn't say it sounded like she'd had anything near a wonderful childhood, she didn't report having had any symptoms that seemed particularly outlandish. I was stunned, then, by her psychiatric diagnosis. She'd been labeled with multiple varieties of depression plus, on top of that, an anxiety disorder.

I asked her more questions to see if maybe there were some dramatic issues she'd left out of her account. She reported some family drama, but nothing that sounded too unusual or insurmountable.

What did I hear when I listened to this young woman? I heard a woman trying desperately to mature, to figure out her life and what she was supposed to be doing with it, to find her place in the universe and her identity as a woman.

Growing up is messy; becoming who we are is difficult; and the work of personal transformation can be some of the hardest work we ever do. But it is not work to be avoided. In Miranda, I saw a person in spiritual crisis, to be sure, but not every spiritual crisis is rightly deemed a "disorder." Sometimes sadness is simply human.

Much to my surprise, her doctors had told her to expect to be on medication for the rest of her life. This seemed unbelievable to me. For more than thirty years, I've had the privilege of counseling people who are going through extreme and seriously traumatic situations. Some have been aided in their healing by the use of pharmaceuticals, and some have not. But something has changed over the past few years. These days, I meet more people whose issues aren't extreme but who nonetheless have been prescribed medication and even told by their doctors and therapists that they may have to be medicated for the foreseeable future, if not forever.

Being human is not a disease. It is full of trials, to be sure, and sometimes those trials are painful. But a knee-jerk pathologizing of emotional pain is a dysfunctional reaction to the experience of being human.

Grief and sadness can be part of a transformational process, one that should not be automatically labeled negative. Difficult emotions are at times appropriate; they can be exactly what we need to experience in order to truly heal, grow, and get to the other side of our suffering with meaningful lessons learned.

In no way is this meant to minimize emotional suffering, or to cast doubt on its debilitating effects. But there are various ways to interpret the source of depression, its meaning, and the best way for dealing with it. Seen through a spiritual lens, depression is the inevitable result of seeing ourselves as separate from the rest of the universe. It is a crisis of the soul.

Yes, it can be painful to face the landscapes of our lives—to remember our childhoods and realize how different they were from how they should have been; to experience the betrayal of friends and loved ones; to reconcile gaps between how we behaved in certain situations and how we later feel we should have behaved; to survive the loss of meaningful work and loving relationships; to endure the abandonment of lovers and spouses; to grieve the death of those we cherished, and so forth.

But such suffering is not transformed by avoiding it or by numbing it. It is transformed when we breathe it in fully, surrendering our minds to the miraculous process by which self-realization and enlightenment emerge from the darkness of our suffering.

In listening to Miranda, I realized that no one had ever suggested any of this to her before. She had never been shown any real reason to hope that a life beyond her sadness was possible without medical intervention. She was trained to see herself as a victim of her condition. And there is something going on here that is a comment on our society today. Seeing deep sadness as a disease, and therefore as something always to be avoided, is an insidious way of trying to avoid that which we most need to address. When we're sad, our task is to deal with the *reason* for the sadness—not just the sadness itself. I did not see Miranda as sick; I saw her as seeking.

To reduce most depression to mere brain chemistry or psychological dynamics is to rob it of its deeper meaning and thus the redemptive potential of its healing. There is a transformational alchemy to the journey out of suffering, sometimes described more powerfully in spiritual than in psychotherapeutic or biological terms. The epidemic of depression we are seeing today should be seen for what it really is: a collective cry for the healing of our hearts.

LETTING SADNESS IN

Many years ago, I *was* Miranda. I was bewildered, lost, and in terrible pain. I cannot imagine where I would be today if the professionals who helped me through my difficulties had told me that I was permanently damaged, as opposed to simply going through a very rough time. At one point I spent a year in tears, but no one threw a bunch of labels at me that would twist my self-perception forever.

During that time, in fact, a friend said to me, "You won't believe this now, Marianne, but one day you will look back on this as having been a good year." I have never forgotten that, because over the years I've come to see the truth in her comment. I now see that period as having been a painful but necessary part of my journey to a functional adulthood. Depression can be a sacred initiation into the journey of enlightenment.

I've always felt that that difficult time in my life was when I became most human. Among other things, it awoke in me a heightened awareness of the pain of others in a way I had not realized before. As the shattered pieces of my own psyche slowly began to come back together, I started wondering whether other people had ever suffered as much as I had, whether anyone else had ever felt such pain.

And what broke through to me very clearly was that, yes, of course they had. Everyone suffers. I had simply been too involved with myself to notice. Never having felt my own pain on such a level, I had no idea what suffering really meant; nor did it ever occur to me that other people feel it too.

Something happens when you realize that if other people have suffered even a fraction as much as you, then they deserve all the compassion you could ever show them and all the effort you could ever make to help them ease their pain.

Such suffering, in all of us, is the result of an excruciating breach between a life of love and life as we have made it. That breach is the cause of all suffering, and closing it is the end to all pain. The breach between ourselves and God, and between ourselves and each other, is the same breach. In closing one, we close the other. Learning how to do this is a spiritual journey.

This journey is a path of self-actualization. In having the courage to face our suffering—to endure it, to learn from it, to process it, to transcend it—we often find keys to living our lives in the most powerful way. As there is mastery in learning how to play the piano or perform any skill, there is mastery in learning how to live life well. And learning how to navigate life's most turbulent moments is simply part of the journey. Few people emerge from the human experience unscathed. Yet we can often gain miraculous insights from our sadness, and avoiding the pain is avoiding the gain.

DRUGS AND THE
SPIRITUAL JOURNEY

Emotional pain is not just a psychological issue; it is a spiritual issue. Depression may or may not be a disease of the brain, but it is definitely a disease of the soul. It isn't something to simply dump in the hands of medical or traditional psychotherapeutic professionals to handle, for how can someone who doesn't recognize the soul be expected to heal it?

The soul, theoretically, is the purview of religion. But in today's society, relatively few people look to religion to truly heal their despair—and for understandable reasons. In most ways organized religion has abdicated its role of spiritual comforter, if not through its own malfeasance, then at least through dissociation from the soulfulness at the core of its mission.

Modern psychotherapy has taken up some of the slack, and yet it too fails to deliver when it doesn't acknowledge the soul work necessary to heal our emotional pain. The psychotherapeutic profession has now turned to the pharmaceutical industry to compensate for its frequent lack of effectiveness, yet the pharmaceutical industry lacks the ability to do much more about our sadness than to numb it.

In the past few years, the medical profession has appropriated the topic of depression, separating the words "sadness" and "depression" in an artificial way that serves no one but the pharmaceutical industry. The idea that a clear line separates the two is a manipulative construct used more to sell medication than to treat a problem. People now talk about "clinical depression" as though there's a blood test to verify it, when in fact there is no such thing. Screening for clinical depression amounts to completing a questionnaire.

Clearly, sometimes people need to seek whatever help they can get, pharmaceutical or otherwise. And treating some mental illnesses—such as bipolar disorder and schizophrenia—with psychotherapeutic drugs can save lives. But although in some cases the use of psychotherapeutic drugs can arguably be a positive, even life-saving regimen, today there is an epidemic of *casual antidepressant use* that most assuredly is not.

According to many experts, clinical depression is being alarmingly overdiagnosed and overtreated. People are offered antidepressants these days—and grab them most readily—as though taking them is no bigger deal than eating a bag of candy. Hundreds of thousands of people simply mention to their healthcare provider once or twice that times have been rough lately and then find themselves with a medical prescription shoved into their hands.

"Perhaps you should be on medication" has become the most common, casual of suggestions, without any serious conversation about exactly what that means. The suggestion comes from doctors, yes, but also from concerned friends and family and media advertising. From seemingly everywhere, we are bombarded by the proposition of happier living through chemistry.

Not everyone going through a rough time—even a very rough time—is mentally ill. It's important not to minimize mental health issues, of course, but it's equally important not to pathologize normal human suffering. The truth is, life can be hard. Growing up is hard, but it's not a mental illness. Divorce is hard, but it's not a mental illness. Grieving the death of a loved one is hard, but it's not a mental illness. If anything should be seen as mental illness, it's the suggestion that all deep suffering is a mental illness.

Some people would argue that any questioning of antidepressant use shows insensitivity toward mental health issues and even ignorance of the need for such medication to help reduce suicide risk. Yet many times people who *were* on antidepressants have committed suicide, and only in very small print is the known link between certain antidepressant use and suicidal ideation made clear. In some cases—*particularly teenagers and young adults*—antidepressants can do more to increase the risk of suicide than to decrease it.

One common refrain I often hear is that "depression is a chemical imbalance." And this often precedes the suggestion that as a chemical condition, depression "requires medication"—though we might question who it is who's doing the requiring. Oncologists don't say chemotherapy is "required," even if they say it is their recommended course of treatment. It might be true that depression is often accompanied by changes in brain chemistry, but that should not automatically be seen as a reason for pharmaceutical intervention. Love, forgiveness, compassion, and prayer cause physiological changes as well. Meditation, for instance, has been shown to alter neurocircuitry and brain wave activity. The automatic assumption that pharmaceuticals are necessary to treat depression is starting to receive the pushback it deserves.

The faux compassion of multibillion-dollar ad campaigns—not just for one antidepressant, mind you, but for that second one you should take on top of that first one (never mind those little risks, such as liver failure!)—is enough to alarm anyone not taking antidepressants. For instance, Abilify (aripiprazole)—currently one of the top-selling prescription drugs in the United States—is classified as an antipsychotic drug. Drug companies now market medicine to the general population that theoretically should be reserved for the very small portion of people with serious mental illness.

Over the past few decades, the use of antidepressants has skyrocketed, particularly among those who have never actually been diagnosed with major mental disorders. Never have Americans been more seriously challenged to think for ourselves. We are becoming psychologically numbed when instead we should be psychologically awakened.

A pharmaceutical-psychotherapeutic-industrial complex now amounts to a sophisticated corporate drug ring, turning intense human suffering into a multibillion-dollar profit center. Moody today? *Here's a mood stabilizer.* Sort of feeling all over the place? *You could be borderline, you know.* Can't sleep? *This could be depression; let's try some medication.* Your mother died? *Let's double your dose for a while.* And the very worst one, the almost criminal marketing pitch masquerading as helpfulness and applied particularly irresponsibly in the lives of our young: *You should expect to be on these for the rest of your life.*

The current trend of easy pill popping lest we shed a tear or two is both psychologically and spiritually unhealthy. It amounts to a societally sanctioned avoidance that keeps us infantilized, emotionally immature, and lacking the skills we need to deal effectively with the critical issues of adult life. It obstructs our capacity for discernment, for perspective, and for real understanding. Most importantly, in separating ourselves from our own pain, we desensitize ourselves to the pain of others; for if I become numb to my own pain, then I am more likely to become numb to yours. And that, in turn, will then cause more pain.

A common justification for casual antidepressant use is that "it takes the edge off" while someone is doing the psychological work. But more often than not, being with the edge until the edge is smoothed out actually *is* the work. Many people are helped by antidepressants today, and for those for whom that is true then I am very glad. But for those who are going through difficult periods of life that are by definition depressing but need not be viewed in pathological terms, there is another way.

RECLAIMING OUR SOULS

The soul is eternally whole and complete in God. An overexternalized worldview separates us from our souls, thus causing us to suffer; and only by reclaiming our souls can we end our suffering. This reclamation of our souls isn't a process of pouring light over the darkness; rather, it is a process of bringing the darkness to light. We must excavate our internal darkness—our barriers to love—for only then can we release them. And none of this necessarily feels good when it's happening.

But in avoiding our sadness we avoid our lives. Learning from our sadness can bear great fruit, and avoiding it can have hidden costs. Our choice is between feeling the sharp pains of self-discovery or enduring the dull ache of unconsciousness that will last for the rest of our lives. Suppressing our pain isn't ending our pain; it's simply displacing it.

The avoidance of sadness decreases our capacity to learn from it. For how can we deeply understand what we have failed to deeply look at? Sometimes it's in the midst of our tears that we come to understand a situation more fully. Even a happy life can have sad days, and sadness is sometimes simply a sign of growth. It doesn't serve any of us to cast a cheap yellow smiley face over almost everything, as though being sad is simply *wrong*. Just as storms have a function in nature, they have a function within the psyche as well. Just as babies who are never exposed to any germs can fail to develop the antibodies they need, people who avoid the fullness of their suffering fail to develop the emotional skills they need to deal with it.

In recognizing the spiritual meaning of our sadness, we find the appropriate place to put it—in our psyches, and in our lives. We come to realize the ways we have separated ourselves from love, from each other, and thus from the peace of God. Knowing this, the true source of our pain, we can then correct the problem on the level where the problem lies.

The "me first" attitude that pervades our society is the source of our epidemic of unhappiness, and collectively changing that attitude is its healing. A society whose entire social and economic system fosters separation from ourselves, from each other, and from the earth on which we live is a society that guarantees suffering. An insane world is telling people who can't align with it that *they* are crazy. Yet finding a way for people to become more easily functional within a dysfunctional society is not a healing of our despair; it's a perverse way of making that despair deeper.

From a spiritual perspective, humanity has a heart disease. To heal a broken leg, we don't just take a painkiller—we have to reset the bone. And to heal our broken hearts, we can't just take a painkiller either—we have to reset our thinking.

SOUL INJURY

The root of most suffering does not lie at the level of brain chemistry but at the level of consciousness, and a scientific worldview that does not acknowledge the power of consciousness cannot fully heal us. Emotional trauma becomes a physical trauma to the brain *because* it is a spiritual trauma.

The severe depression of a returning war veteran, for instance, is sometimes due to brain injury—but not always. It is often primarily due to *soul* injury. When a young person has been injured in war, when people have tried to kill him, when he has witnessed the horrors of battle, and when he has been trained to be a killing machine and to live with the aftermath of what he might have had to do—how can his soul *not* suffer? The grieving mother of a soldier who had recently committed suicide—a young man I had once known as a funny, brilliant kid so filled with a zest for life I was sure he would do great things someday—said to me through her tears, "Oh Marianne, they tried to turn him into someone I didn't raise him to be." They had to, of course, but what a tragedy this leaves us with.

All of us wish to see our suffering veterans healed. And there are extraordinary professionals throughout our country working with them, and healing them, in a myriad of ways. But those who would argue that a widespread use of antidepressants among our veterans is necessary given the high suicide rate among them (almost one every hour, according to a 2013 investigation by the Department of Veterans Affairs) might consider the countervailing factor of a known suicide risk among people who take antidepressants. This risk applies particularly to those age twenty-nine or younger, which includes the vast majority of our veterans. No external medicine alone can solve the problems of memories such as those dealt with by our returning soldiers.

These men and women need spiritual medicine, which means not only the comfort of God, but also the love of their fellow human beings. They need human kindness, prayer, therapy, meditation, a society that proves through economic and social policies toward veterans that it actually gives a damn (not just political rhetoric and easy words like "Thank you for your service"), perhaps an apology for having sent so many of them to wars that never should have been fought, and some sign—anywhere—that we are seriously considering alternatives to war.

Spirituality isn't some quaint stepchild of an intelligent worldview, or the only option for those of us not smart enough to understand the facts of the real world. Spirituality reflects the most sophisticated mindset and the most powerful force available for the transformation of human suffering—whether someone is taking medication or not. That is why learning the basics of a spiritual worldview—and the mental, emotional, and behavioral principles that this entails—is key to reclaiming our inner peace.

Darkness cannot exist in the presence of light. Meditation is a path to light. Forgiveness is a key to light. Prayer is a path to light. Those are powers that give comfort to the soul, providing what no earthly remedy can. And they are the powers we most need to develop now. They heal our lives by healing our thoughts; and it is in learning to change our thinking that we learn to change our lives. As it is written in Romans 12:2, "Be transformed by the renewing of your mind." Renewing our minds, we will renew the world.

FOUR

The Miraculous Universe

*L*earning the basic tenets of the spiritual universe is the first step
in the path to enlightenment. First we learn the principles; then
we go through the process of trying to apply them in both our personal and collective experience.

Everyone is on a spiritual journey; most people just don't know
it. Spirituality refers not to some theological dynamic outside ourselves, but to how we choose to use our minds. The spiritual path
is the path of the heart; at every moment, we're either walking the
path of love and creating happiness, or swerving from it and creating suffering. Every thought we think leads deeper into love or
deeper into fear.

Love is sane, and fear is not. The loving mind is the "right mind";
the word "right-eous" refers to "right use." In the words of Mahatma

Gandhi, "The problem with the world today is that humanity is not in its right mind."

The spiritual universe is the Mind of God. Miracles are the thoughts of love, extended from the Mind of God through the mind of humans and out into the world. God is Love, and as God's children, so are we. Our purpose on earth is to think as God thinks, which means to love as God loves. When our minds are attuned to love, things unfold miraculously. Loving thought creates loving feelings, and loving feelings create loving behavior. In this way we create happiness for ourselves and for those around us.

Obviously, life doesn't always go like that. But it should. For love is in fact our natural state, from which we have veered as a species and to which all of us long to return. In ways both large and small—from the small deviations from love that mar the landscapes of our personal relationships, to the horrors of war and genocide—humanity plays out a spiritual love/hate relationship with our true selves. We're one with love, we turn away from love, and ultimately we return to love. That's pretty much all there is.

When our minds are not attuned to love, the natural fabric of the universe is rent. But the universe is both self-organizing and self-correcting. When lost in the illusion of fear, we can return to love and thus return to peace. Each of us has been imbued with an Internal Teacher, a guide who's been authorized by God to pave a path home for us when we're lost in the pain of worldly illusion. We can call this force by many names (one of which is the Holy Spirit), but we cannot call on it in vain.

The miracle is a divine intercession on behalf of our spirit, restoring the celestial order. Miracles break us free of chains that otherwise bind us by lifting us above the fixed limitations of the mortal world. The ego's chains are not material, but mental; they're simply our fixed beliefs about the three-dimensional world. By transitioning from faith in the power of our disasters to faith in the power of God to heal them, we release the power of miracles to work on our behalf.

But in order to work miracles, good intentions are not enough. We need to do more than *intend* to see things differently; we must be *willing* to see things differently. "Dear God, I am willing to see this differently" is the most powerful prayer for miraculous transformation. Where the ego insists that the world should be different, the spirit seeks to see the world differently. Only then does the world really change. We can't ask God for the "miracle" of things happening the way we want them to happen; the miracle is when we *think* about things the way God would have us think about them.

Spirit blesses, while the ego blames. Spirit forgives, while the ego attacks. Spirit allows, while the ego defends. Spirit is fully available in the present, while the ego is attached to past or future. In every moment we make a decision, consciously or unconsciously, whether to be host to God or hostage to the ego.

And the choice isn't always easy. Your spouse has left you after twenty-five years—where is the miracle there? Your child has died of a drug overdose—where is the miracle there? You have lost your job and don't know how you'll support your family—where is the miracle there? Your doctor says you have only six months to live—where is the miracle there? You don't know whether you'll get the use of your legs back—where is the miracle there? You can't escape the memories of past trauma—where is the miracle there?

The world will offer you many ways to numb your pain, to fortify your anger, and thus to deepen your despair. You can always find people to agree with you that you've been victimized, and on the mortal plane, you may have been. You can always find people to agree with you that a situation is hopeless, and from a rational perspective, it might seem that way. All of us to a greater or lesser degree go through experiences about which, from a worldly perspective, we have every right to feel angry, victimized, or agonizingly hopeless.

Yet even then we have a choice. We can build a case against those who hurt us—dooming ourselves to pain and self-pity. We can insist that no matter what anyone says, there is no hope in a situation going forward—dooming ourselves to complete despair. We can face the world with negativity and blame, defensiveness and attack, condemnation and anger—dooming ourselves to a cold and isolated existence.

Or we can have a miracle instead.

This choice to see a miracle means repudiating the ego's thought system. It is the choice to stand our attitudinal ground despite the ego's insistence that we're at the mercy of a fear-laden world. This is the metaphysical meaning of Jesus's words, "Satan, get thee behind me." Your feelings of hopelessness are the ego's prize, the pathways of its dark and bitter kingdom. But with God's help you can rise above the ego. His light dispels the darkness and delivers us from the pain we feel there. He lifts us above the torment and the agony of the ego's world.

I once asked a woman whose husband had left her what she thought might make her feel better, and her response was threefold: that her estranged husband's new relationship would fail; that he would wake up and realize that he'd been a fool and would return to her; or that something awful would happen to him or to the new woman in his life! She laughed, but she was crying too.

All of us on some level can understand her answer. But in truth, such thoughts as those will only exacerbate her pain. The most powerful thought is a prayerful thought. When I'm praying for you, I'm praying for my own peace of mind. I can only have for myself what I am willing to wish for you.

I asked this woman whether she'd like a prayerful alternative to her current thoughts about her husband. And her response was perfect: "If a prayer might release me from the hell I'm in, then please, let's say it."

Dear God,

Please bless my former love,

Who has decided to move away from me.

Despite my resistance, I bless his path

And pray that he be happy.

Remove my temptation to judge him

Or to control him,

For binding him to my judgment

But binds me to my suffering.

Help me to forgive him, God,

And thus forgive myself.

Free him from my hooks, dear God,

And free me from my pain.

Amen

Prayer is the conduit of miracles. It shifts the universe by shifting us. The ego has an endless array of options by which to treat the problems it creates. But none of them do anything but drive us deeper into despair. One thing the ego will never suggest is that love is always the answer, because love is the ego's dissolution and it knows it. It feeds on lovelessness for its survival, yet *its* survival is *our* destruction.

The ego views forgiveness as weakness and attack as strength. But love is not weakness; it is the power of God. The problem isn't whether or not love works miracles; the problem is how much we resist love.

It's easy enough to have faith in love when everyone around us is being nice and things are going the way we want them to. But life is a learning process through which we're constantly challenged to love more deeply. The universe is intentional and will not be done with us until we've gotten to the place where love, and only love, is our reality. We're not on this earth to just hang around; we're here to actualize our enlightened potential. And the universe will make sure we do.

So yes, people will be unkind to us; and yes, things won't always turn out the way we wish; and yes, there are tragedies in the world. But God's store of miracles is infinite, and by standing for love we learn to call them forth. There is nothing that our holiness, or "whole mind," cannot do. Holiness is the embodiment of the love that transforms all those experiences and releases us from our torment.

The search for holiness isn't pink and gauzy; it's tough and gritty. We don't pretend not to be angry when we're angry; we surrender our anger into the hands of God and tell Him we're willing not to be. We don't deny our tears when we've been abandoned or betrayed; we pray for the happiness of the person who hurt us, as an act of generosity toward ourselves. We don't pretend that we're not afraid or lonely; we place our fear and loneliness in God's hands. All of this is a process and none of it is easy. Many tears have lined the paths of saints.

But God is with us during the difficult times as much as during any other. As we walk through the darkest nights of our souls, we are bolstered, should we care to be, by the power of faith that we are not alone.

FAITH

During times of emotional darkness, what does it actually mean to have faith?

Faith is a unique psychological orientation, a powerful reminder of the light of God that exists beyond the darkness. Faith helps us during periods of depression and sadness because it gives us the patience to endure. We understand that if we do the inner work, the work will pay off. Faith isn't blind, it's visionary. A pilot who cannot see the horizon does not conclude that the horizon isn't there. Faith is like the pilot then flying on instruments. As the Bible tells us, "Blessed are those who do not see but have faith anyway."

Faith is an aspect of consciousness; we're constantly applying our faith to one world or the other. Our problem is that we tend to have more faith in the power of cancer to kill us than we have faith in the power of God to heal us.

There's a divine order to the spiritual universe, and chaos of any kind is temporary. Faith is simply recognizing this. Whatever the ego casts down, God will ultimately lift back up. This is not just a belief; it's spiritual intelligence. And spiritual intelligence gives us strength and fortitude. Faith as a container for our emotions is important because it gives us certainty in the face of uncertainty. During times of suffering it keeps us above the emotional waterline, giving us the strength to endure by knowing that whatever it is, this too shall pass. There is a huge emotional difference between "I'm depressed and I feel like this pain will never end" and "I'm depressed but I know that I'll get through this." It can be very dark on certain nights, but there is no question whether dawn will come. No matter what has happened in our lives, miracles are possible. The universe works like a GPS. Even if a wrong turn gets taken on the way to your destination, the GPS will simply recalibrate and provide another route. The destination is inner peace. Tough times occur, but they ultimately cannot and will not last as long as we choose love.

GOD'S INTELLIGENCE

The universe is alive, imbued with a natural intelligence guiding all things toward their highest good. This intelligence turns an embryo into a baby, a bud into a blossom, and an acorn into an oak tree. When we allow it to, it guides us to becoming the highest version of ourselves, living lives of happiness and peace. Learning how to align ourselves with this natural intelligence is the most intelligent thing we can possibly do.

In the Introduction to *A Course in Miracles,* it is written:

> Nothing real can be threatened.
> Nothing unreal exists.
> *Herein lies the peace of God.*

Only love is ultimately real, and anything else is a temporary illusion manufactured by the mind. What is not love does not actually exist.

Obviously, such thinking runs counter to material evidence. Looking around, we perceive the world with our physical senses—all of which report that the world is very real indeed. Yet what the body's senses report to us as "real world" is in fact a giant, collective, mortal hallucination. In the words of Albert Einstein, "Reality is merely an illusion, albeit a very persistent one." The material world is but a veil in front of a world that is more true, more real, more beautiful. It is a vast veil of illusion, created by the ego not to illuminate, but to hide, the world that lies beyond it.

Everything that causes us to suffer—from the most heinous abuses to the loss of a loved one—is happening within a realm of illusion. Such suffering is our human experience and should be respected as such, but the human experience alone is not the ultimate truth of who we are. We are beings of a world more real than this one; it is the world beyond the veil. The spiritual world is a universe of love and love only, where nothing but eternal peace and harmony exist.

The self that suffers, therefore, is not the real you. The world can throw terrible things your way, but it cannot change the reality of who you are. Who you really are is a being of love, completely unaffected by the lovelessness of the world.

The journey of enlightenment is a journey to a transformed sense of self, a conversion to a different sense of who we are and what the world is for. Although the ego argues that we are limited, guilty, temporary, vulnerable beings grasping for little bits of happiness within a world of scarcity, a spiritual worldview says we are none of those things. In God, we are innocent. We are abundant. We are complete. We are eternal.

And in remembering these things, we are happy at last. For they are more than abstractions. They are explosions of light.

CLOSING THE GAP

The mortal self—defined by the body, described in terms of worldly circumstances, and at the effect of the material world—is but an aspect of who we are. In fact, the body is like a wall we have built around an invisible self. That invisible self—be it called the Christ, or Buddha Mind, or *shekinah*, or by any other name—is who we essentially, fundamentally, and eternally are. You are not a body, but an eternal spirit. You were alive before your physical birth, and you will be alive beyond your physical death. What God creates cannot be uncreated.

It is a radical commitment to try to remember who we are in a world that does all it can, every moment of every day, to persuade us that we are who we really aren't and that we aren't who we really are. The world as we know it is organized around the denial of spiritual sight, treating bodies as real and spirit as fantasy. It rests on the pre-supposition that only what happens externally matters. As such, our modern civilization is spiritually blind. It is ignorant of the deeper reality and meaning of life. It is asleep to the deeper dynamics and evolutionary imperatives of human existence, and in its sleep it has produced nightmares for individuals and for the entire species.

The ravages produced by our spiritual ignorance are now being experienced on massive scales, producing deep psychological and emotional problems in individuals and seemingly unstoppable environmental and political destructiveness in the world. But such problems are not causes; they are effects that have resulted from a state of humanity in which we have become dissociated from what we truly are. Separated from who we are, we become neurotic at best and genuinely insane at worst.

The ego mind, the delusional self, seeks every moment of every day to annihilate God's creation. Which means its goal is to annihilate *you*. Within this world, the ego can have devastating effects. All of this is happening within a vast illusion, but the effects of the illusion feel very real while we are in the midst of it. The role of the miracle-worker is not to ignore the darkness but to dispel it.

The ego's world is as depressing as it is insane, of course. It posits us as temporary beings, when in fact we're eternal. It posits us as separate from God, when in fact we are thoughts within His Mind. It posits us as separate from each other, when in fact we are created as one and remain as one. To heal our depression, we must close the mental gap between that which is the ego's view of ourselves and others, and God's view of ourselves and others. This is the only salvation from sadness and pain.

The ego is our own mental energy turned against us. Yet just as darkness is nothing but the absence of light, so fear is nothing but the absence of love. The ego is simply a mental miscreation, the delusional thought that we are not who in fact we are. In its mad belief that we are separate, it persuades us that we are alone . . . and endangered . . . and unloved. *Of course* we are depressed. And the healing of our depression lies in remembering who we are.

We are perfect, innocent children of God. That is God's Reality, and God's Reality is changeless. Moreover, we were created as one and on the level of spirit we *are* one. The ego is vigilant in its efforts to make us forget we are perfect, to make us forget we are innocent, and to make us forget we are one. The anxiety and mental anguish this forgetfulness produces is the real meaning of the word "hell." The awareness of our oneness and the peace this produces is the meaning of the word "heaven." Hell is not our natural habitat. Heaven is where we come from and where we belong—not just after we die, but every moment of every day.

THE GREAT LIE

Henry David Thoreau wrote that "the mass of men lead lives of quiet desperation." From a spiritual perspective, that despair is rooted in a delusion: the inaccurate perception that any part of life is separate from any other part. The misperception is maintained by the evidence of the physical senses, which experience reality in physical rather than spiritual terms, thus positing us as separate when in fact we are not. This central, pernicious belief in separation obliterates love and induces fear, by leading us to experience ourselves as separate from what, and from whom, we cannot in fact be separate. This delusion is the source of our despair because, on the level of thought, it cuts the oneness of our being into billions of separate pieces and thus violates our most fundamental sense of self.

We are, according to *A Course in Miracles,* like sunbeams thinking we are separate from the sun or waves in the ocean thinking we're separate from other waves. Let's consider what that means psychologically. If I'm a wave in the ocean and I think I'm separate from all the other waves, then how could I not be afraid of the ocean? How could I not feel powerless? How could I not be terrified that at any moment I might be overwhelmed by other waves? But if I think of myself as I really am—not separate at all from other waves—then I know that I am safe in the ocean and that the power of the ocean is my power too.

All suffering derives from our false attachment to the kingdom of the personal self. Pain is inevitable as long as we see ourselves as separate from the rest of life. Cells in the body that separate from their natural intelligence, forgetting their function and going off to form their own kingdoms, are called cancer cells. They're malignant, having broken off from the great collaborative dance of life. And that is what has happened to humanity; we've been infected by a spiritual malignancy, in which, like cancer cells, we've forgotten that our function is to collaborate with other cells in order to foster the greater life of which we are all a part. Instead, we've been led to believe that there is no higher good than doing whatever we want to do—with no sense of greater responsibility to the whole of which we are part. And the power with which we are intended to create becomes a power by which we destroy.

Fearful attitudes, rooted in the belief in separation and forming a social toxicity that is poisoning our world, pervade every aspect of our society. Such toxicity is destructive to our psyches and even to our bodies. Whether it's violence on TV or the violence of war, conflict between neighbors or conflict between races, it feels at times as though fear is everywhere and love is practically nowhere.

We grasp for love as though we're gasping for air, yet too often we cannot find it. We're lured into false beliefs about who we are and who we are to each other—essentially believing that we are ultimately nothing and we are nothing to each other; such beliefs accumulate to the point of becoming a massive, unquestioned lie that spreads across the consciousness of humanity like a blanket of doom. The lie is fortified so completely, so constantly, and so chronically that it seems like it must be true. But a ubiquitous lie is still a lie.

The lie is fortified everywhere. Our religions, our economies, our nationalities, our sexualities, our politics, our cultures: the ego uses all as evidence of our separateness and warns us constantly, "Do not trust each other!" We are *taught* to fear rather than to love one another. We perceive a world of scarcity—of lack, of danger—and from that perception we conclude that we must compete to get our needs met at the expense of whomever else. In truth, it is our perception of separation that creates the scarcity to begin with.

So what is the source of the lie, and how can it be removed? The truth is, it comes from no specific place because it comes from everywhere. It is simply human consciousness devoid of love. The ego mind is the psychological meaning of the devil's lair, but there is no physical devil's lair where all the lies of the world are concocted. Fear is the power of our minds turned against ourselves—the loveless, disassociated, despairing self. It's our self-hatred posing as self-love.

Given the fact that fear rather than love prevails within the dominant thought system on the planet today, it is not surprising that so many of us are depressed: the organizing principles of modern civilization dislodge us spiritually from our place in the universe. A fear-based, materially obsessed mentality has leached a sense of spiritual purpose from the bones of our civilization, and this *hurts* us.

We do not—and cannot—emotionally fit into a world in which no transcendent meaning is ascribed to the experience of being human; in which no deep connection or mutual responsibility is presupposed in our connection to other living things; in which more forces exist to separate us than to unite us; and in which our worth is determined primarily by external factors. This maelstrom of diseased thinking—diseased in that none of it fosters love and all of it fosters fear—has turned our civilization into a petri dish of social pathology. It is a collective problem whose consequences we experience on an individual level.

And how could it be otherwise? How could a civilization that so marginalizes love *not* leave people heartbroken? The deep emotional suffering so rampant among us is a disease of the spirit and will not be healed on a material level. It will be healed only when addressed on a spiritual level.

A spiritual disease demands a spiritual solution, and a spiritual solution does not numb or avoid our suffering. To numb or avoid suffering is to fail to expose its source to the light of conscious awareness. If we are unaware of our pain, we cannot surrender it, and only pain surrendered is pain dissolved.

God will not take from us what we will not release to Him; to do so would be to violate our free will. Spiritual toxins must be brought to the surface in order to be released. They are released as a part of an emotional detoxification process, without which they remain within us to damage our lives. Our modern worldview does not recognize the emotional toxicity at its core. Our mechanistic, rationalistic, overly secularized *worldview* is toxic; therefore, our worldview needs to be healed before our suffering can be.

THE PATH TO HEALING

The genius of nature applies to both body and mind.

This extraordinary natural intelligence is obvious in the workings of our biological systems. In the creation of the human body, egg and sperm are first joined in a cellular marriage out of which arises a mind-boggling process of cell creation and division. Cells emerge and divide to become muscles, skin, organs, and blood. Brains, lungs, livers, hearts, fingernails, genitals, eyeballs, tongues, toes—all develop from billions and billions of tiny cells that are guided to collaborate with other cells in an infinitely creative process leading to the birth of a baby. Then, even after the birth, these processes continue in a way that supports the body in functioning and thriving as an independent being.

Notice that at no time does nature rely on you or me to do any of that. *We ourselves did not author this process.* The natural intelligence guiding our biological functioning simply *is.* And whether we think of this genius in spiritual or secular terms, the point is that this same genius applies to our psychological and emotional functioning as well. Just as biologically we are programmed to be born, spiritually we are programmed to be happy. Divine intelligence but uses the body as a means to a more creative end.

This is nature's intention and the purpose of our lives: that we grow and thrive not only biologically, but also spiritually. Nature's intelligence leads us to our highest creativity, goodness, and joy. The issue isn't whether or not this intelligence exists, but only whether or not we follow it. Connected to that intelligence, which is love itself, we are guided to wholeness and inner peace. Disconnected from it, we are guided by ego into the darkness of chaos and pain. Free will simply means that the choice is up to us.

The mind is part of a perfectly orchestrated ecosystem, just as is the physical body. It has inbuilt mechanisms of survival, just as does the physical body. And it has ways to repair itself, just as does the physical body. The body would not survive were it not able to absorb a certain amount of injury, and neither would the mind. Both are imbued with brilliant immune systems, mechanisms of repair by which they heal injury and resist disease.

When we suffer an emotional trauma, we might feel as though we've been beaten up—because in a way we have been, either by ourselves, by others, or by life. Our inner selves have been bruised, and we need time to heal. When healing physically, we need to be gentle with our bodies; when healing emotionally, we need to be gentle with our hearts. Anyone who is depressed understands that the inner self can be in pain as great as any pain of the physical body.

A certain amount of sickness and pain is simply a part of life, and a certain amount of heartbreak is a part of life as well. It takes time to recover from a physical injury, and it takes time to recover from an emotional one. Our understanding this, and allowing for it, is simply part of living wisely. The period of time during which the mind is absorbing and processing loss, disappointment, and fear is not a disease. Feeling that loss, disappointment, and fear doesn't necessarily mean that something is *wrong*. It simply means we are bruised and need time to heal.

People didn't just start dying recently. People didn't just start experiencing catastrophic situations recently. People didn't just start enduring heartbreak recently. Over time, when faced with challenges and threats to our survival, we have adapted to meet threats on both external and internal levels. Both body and mind have developed immune systems, and the basis of the mind's immune system is grief. Grief allows us to process incrementally what might be too shocking to the system to have to process all at once.

Grief over the normal losses of life should not be avoided, but accepted and embraced. It is a process—not an event—best served when we surrender to it fully. When our feelings have been deeply hurt, we need to settle into what might be a painful period with full understanding that this is going to be hard but we will get through it. We need to stock up on whatever helps us make it through; and gather people around us who are healthy, supportive, compassionate companions while we process our loss and move through our feelings. The grief will come in waves, and it will take as long as it takes. The last thing we need to do is tell ourselves to hurry, to get on with it, to push through, to "get over it." We wouldn't do that with our bodies, and we shouldn't do it with our souls.

One of the neuroses of modernity is the impulse to rush what should not be rushed. We have taken the dictates of a business model and imposed them onto everything. If something makes us less "productive" for a period of time, then surely something must be wrong. But ultimately, what could be more *productive* than moving beyond deep debilitating sorrow and reclaiming our inner peace?

The right time to be heartbroken is when the heart is breaking. Just as an expectant mother sometimes serves her pregnancy best by resting comfortably, her feet up and drinking a cup of chamomile tea; so during times of grief we, too, are gestating the next phase of our lives and serve the process best simply by allowing it to be. We need to rest into who we are and where we are; in being gentle with ourselves, we make greater space for the gigantic processes of personal transformation that are occurring deep inside us. Spiritually, we are always dying and we are always being born.

Feeling appropriate respect for grief, we give ourselves greater permission to go through it. I remember when far more credence was given to the experience of deep grief; people weren't expected to simply bounce back quickly after the death of a loved one. Family members might have worn black (which was unusual back then) for a year to signal their mourning. It was simply understood that people wouldn't be themselves for a while, and they felt *permission* to not be themselves. Today, people are apt to feel guilty for grieving, after someone says to them: "It's been a month since your mother died. Aren't you *over* it yet?" At such a time, it's more than okay— in fact, it's very healthy—to say, "No, I'm not, and I probably *won't* be for a while."

We are not machines. We are human beings. And when we're grieving, we're moving through a profound and significant experience. A sorrowful time can be a sacred time. Respecting the heart when we are in pain, seeking to walk through the experience very close to God, doesn't immediately make us less sad; but it makes our sadness begin to make sense. Dwelling in a sacred universe gives us a different emotional perspective, one in which life is ascribed a deeper meaning because we choose to see it from a deeper perspective. We choose to see all things, even our suffering, within the context of how deeply we might learn to love.

No matter what happens in life, it is our choice whether to play it deep or to play it shallow. And whenever we play life deep, we feel our feelings deeply. Times of great sadness might open up painful wounds that were buried before. They might be wounds that are not just ours, but generational or societal. Suffering through them with our hearts wide open is not for sissies, but for seekers. Those wounds were keeping us from being who we're capable of being, and their coming up to be healed is part of our journey to enlightenment.

During that process, if we are forced to burn through what might seem at times like unbearable pain, we might weep. And that's okay.

FIVE

A Culture of Depression

*T*here exists a spiritual vacuum at the heart of our society, the natural consequence of which is a low-level sadness. The very worldview that permeates our civilization is depressing. A mechanistic interpretation of the world teaches us to see people as machines, not as multidimensional beings—as bodies, but not as spirits. This mindset denies who and what we actually are. We live with endless, tiny repudiations of our true nature throughout the day every day of our lives.

Simply living in today's world is emotionally traumatic. But our emotional disconnection from each other, from ourselves, from nature, from God—indeed, from any sense of transcendent reality—is not one specific violent event. Rather, it is the consistent, rolling trauma of living in a world so disconnected from love. We are not just depressed about specific incidents, and we are not just depressed as individuals. We are depressed collectively.

Collective issues run through our personal dramas:

~ Someone is depressed over a breakup or divorce. *The collective issue is, why do we commonly find relationships so hard to make work?*

~ Someone is depressed over the loss of a loved one. *The collective issue is, why do we give ourselves so little permission to grieve?*

~ Someone is depressed over the loss of money or career. *The collective question is, why have we acquiesced to the creation of an economy in which the majority of people are so financially squeezed?*

~ Someone is depressed over a child having died of a drug overdose. *The collective issue is, what kind of society have we created that so many young people are rushing to drugs to begin with?*

~ Someone is depressed over past trauma or abuse. *The collective issue is, what is the spiritual vacuum at the heart of our society that so little attention, comfort, hope, and inspiration are available to those who suffer?*

Yes, we have an epidemic of depression in our society today. But truthfully, how could anyone today on some level *not* be sad? The gap between how beautiful life can be and the way it too often is is heartbreaking. Anyone who is not on some level grieving the state of the world is perhaps not looking very deeply.

Sometimes the source of our personal despair is actually a proxy for a more collective upset. What causes our pain might be personal, but the pain itself is universal. Just as for millennia Greeks and Romans and European explorers did not know the source of the Nile River, no one today can quite name the specific source of the free-floating despair so prevalent among us. Depression is caused by trauma that separates spirit from personality, yet the trauma is not always triggered by a particular event.

None of our lives can be fully understood outside the context of the general state of humanity any more than a child's life can be fully understood outside the context of that child's family system. Human beheadings blaring at us from video screens bring horror to our doorsteps whether we live in Iraq or in Illinois. It can't honestly be said about anyone anymore, "Well, what have *you* got to be sad about?" Much of the world is crying out in pain that most all of us feel on some level.

We're depressed because life today is *off*. We're depressed because too often we have no sense of our place in the universe, our relationship to the source of our existence, a deeper sense of purpose in our relationships with other human beings, or any sense of reverence toward any aspect of life at all. Our entire civilization is ruled more by fear than by love.

We are experiencing an unsustainable breach between the knowledge of the heart and the experience of being human. This throws us into the quiet hysteria of existential crisis, and it is that crisis—not just its symptoms—that needs to be seriously addressed.

The crisis of modern society is that human beings too often feel spiritually homeless within it. And how could it be otherwise? How could the soul feel at home on our planet, given the soullessness of our civilization? With a barrage of discordant information bombarding us constantly—ranging from the utterly meaningless to the hideously violent—where is the heart to seek comfort? The issue is not only that Sheila is depressed, or Robert is depressed; the issue is that our culture itself is in too many ways depressing.

A society that exalts the accumulation of wealth but diminishes the relevance of wisdom, that exalts the power of force but diminishes the power of love, is a society that has lost touch with its soul. And living within that society, we can too easily lose touch with ours.

This collective depression is so huge, so all-pervasive that few people even recognize how strange it is. It is like a toxic gas that almost everyone is inhaling. Most people, if they were to describe their depression, would speak of a feeling that almost everyone has known at one time or another. The vast majority of people who when asked "How are you?" respond by saying "Fine," are lying.

The organizational principles that rule our civilization are inherently pathological, constantly pitting us against ourselves, and against each other, in ways both large and small.

First, we're told that value lies outside ourselves, in material things rather than in who we are. This is a direct contradiction of the spiritual value inherent in every creation of God.

Second, we're taught to think that promoting ourselves at the expense of others is natural and even good. This puts us at odds with our deeper selves, because the spirit cannot *help* but care deeply about the suffering of others.

Third, we're trained by a dominant worldview not so much to relate to other people as to merely transact with them—even then, not for the sake of genuine communion, but for the purpose of getting what we think we want from them.

Psychically, these twisted perceptions are tearing us apart.

An all-pervasive disregard for the reality of the inner self is a setup for despair. Our societal perspective desensitizes us to both our own deeper needs and the needs of others. And the two together form a toxic brew now threatening the fabric of our civilization. The fact that this brew is causing havoc in your life, or in mine, is almost secondary to the fact that it's causing havoc for the human race.

PERSONAL AND COLLECTIVE DEPRESSION

Just as enlightenment is the antidote to individual despair, it is the antidote to our collective despair as well. The spiritual journey is not limited to the path of the individual. We're challenged not just as individuals, but as nations, as groups, and ultimately as a species to become the embodiment of our more loving selves.

All of us, in order to be fully conscious, are now asked to address larger issues regarding not only who we are as individuals, but also who we are as a civilization. We are asked to meet the challenge of an evolutionary crisis now facing the entire species. For our collective challenges will affect all of us in time.

It's tempting to focus on an individual's experience of depression, while avoiding larger factors that make their despair more probable.

The incidence of domestic violence, for instance, increases with the presence of poverty. The incidence of street crime is increased by high unemployment. The extreme financial stress that so many experience is largely due to a rigged financial system. Certain health issues derive from an inadequate healthcare system and a recklessness toward our environment. Millions of young people lose opportunities for higher education and economic advancement for no other reason than that we put the economic good of banks before the economic potential of our young.

Many of our personal woes derive from social policies that are spiritually diseased—diseased in that they fail to reflect an awareness of our oneness. The disease in the policy then infects the individual, whose emotional disease is then called depression. But the larger epidemic of individual fatigue, weariness, and lack of vitality will not be adequately assuaged until we address the larger problems in our society. Behind every newly depressed person will be another, until all of us wake up and realize that this problem should be more than a goldmine for drug manufacturers.

Even when we're depressed about specific problems—related to money, relationships, illness, and so forth—such causes often emerge from a larger matrix of societal dysfunction. While it's important to take personal responsibility for our own lives, it's also important to be alert to societal factors that increase or decrease the probability of personal hardship. The two in fact cannot be meaningfully separated. Our tendency over the past century to separate the experience of the individual from the experience of the collective has created blind spots in our view of both.

Dividing personal from collective anxiety—categorizing them as two distinctly separate issues—is an inadequate way to address what is deeply wrong in the world today. The more we understand a larger social context for our problems, the more empowered we can be in addressing them. This is where modern psychotherapy, with its emphasis on the individual sufferer, has exacerbated as much as helped to heal the problem. The last thing we need to be, when depressed, is focused only on ourselves. First of all, it's in reaching out to others that we summon the love that creates miracles. And second, how is it relevant how my parents behaved when I was a child but not relevant how larger pressures weighed upon them and stressed them to the breaking point? Understanding deeper emotional realities can and should give us deeper insight into societal issues, and vice versa. If I understand, for instance, that my mother ignored me emotionally after the birth of my younger sibling, it's important to realize the stress that she was under. If it had to do with her having limited time at home, then I can understand more deeply why laws such as paid maternity leave matter. By becoming an advocate for paid maternity leave, I'm helping to save other mothers and children from the stress that my mother and I went through many years before. Most importantly, doing what I can do to generate new hope, not only for myself, but also for other people— reaching out to others, participating in creating larger societal solutions—helps me move beyond my own suffering. Hope is born of participation in hopeful solutions. One of the most dysfunctional attitudes we have toward emotional suffering today is that the sufferer is always alone in their suffering. We are not alone—we are all recipients of psychologically poisonous messages about who we are and why we are here. Our pain is shared by others whose lives are similarly ripped apart by the inevitable dysfunctions of a spiritually ambivalent civilization. The highest spiritual law is to love thy neighbor as thyself. The world is divided today as never before between two major groups: those who think we should, and those who think we shouldn't.

It's very important, when we are deeply sad, to take a stand against the part of the mind that says, "This is only about you." Nothing is ever "only about you" for *you yourself are not only about you*. All of us are part of a larger whole, a larger humanity, and all miracles derive from knowing that. The subconscious mind does not recognize us as separate from each other—because we're not. We heal the wounds of the past through healing in the present, and we heal our own broken hearts by reaching out to the hearts of others. The moment I become part of a larger solution, and a larger world, my own healing begins. We should make time to be alone and cry, yes, but we should also make time to put on a courageous smile for those whose problems are as big or even bigger than ours. There are a lot of hours in every day.

Years ago, I led support groups for people dealing with AIDS. One day a young man said to me, "I won't be coming to the group today because I don't need support. I had a good week this week."

I responded, "Well maybe this week it's your turn to be there and support someone who didn't." I saw on his face that my comment didn't bother him; it empowered him. Throughout the AIDS crisis I saw the miraculous effects of a community filled with individual sufferers, which yet came together with so much love among its members that even an experience of the deepest darkness contained moments of inexpressible light.

THE PASSION CURE

How often I've heard a variation on this theme: "I used to believe in God, but I can't now. How could a loving God let children starve?" The answer, of course, is that God doesn't let children starve; we do. The biggest problems in the world today are not of God's making, but of ours. And we keep making them.

~ A world in which young people are subjected to violent images on video screens almost all day long is a world in which they are more apt to become depressed.

~ A world in which young people grow up pressured to learn at school in a specified manner regardless of whether their brains function that way is a world in which they are more apt to become depressed.

~ A world in which young people are more likely than not to experience a home life dominated by their parents' economic stresses is a world in which they are more apt to become depressed.

~ A world in which young people are aware that environmental destructiveness, permanent war machinery, an unjust economic system, and an increasingly unjust criminal justice system undergird our social and political systems is a world in which they are more apt to become depressed.

~ A world in which young people see exorbitant costs of higher education and lack of economic opportunity looming large in their futures is a world in which they are more apt to become depressed.

When ten-year-olds are becoming depressed, we have a problem that goes way beyond that household. Such children are reflecting Mommy and Daddy's stress, which is reflecting relationship issues or economic issues or other factors that reflect humanity's having mislaid its soul.

The suffering of our children should be an arrow that pierces the shield of our denial and alerts us to what is happening in the world. The depressed among us are like dead canaries in a coal mine, revealing a terrible toxin that will kill us all if we go down the shaft.

Yet we continue to go down, rarely questioning the toxicity of the mine. Why? Because an insane order of things tells us that there is nothing wrong with the mine; there's simply something wrong with the canaries!

We do all this to avoid the pain of looking at our pain. An overly externalized worldview doesn't know how to treat internal pain except through external means—seeking to eradicate or suppress symptoms, but not necessarily dealing with their cause. The cause, however, will be suppressed for only so long before morphing into another kind of symptom.

Psychic pain, like physical pain, is there for a reason. It is not an illness; it is a messenger—a messenger we too often choose to ignore. *A Course in Miracles* says it is not up to us what we learn but only whether we learn through joy or pain. This applies to a civilization as much as to an individual. If something is happening, it's happening whether or not we're choosing to reflect upon its meaning. But we will reflect upon the meaning of so much unnecessary suffering in the world today, or we will pay a very, very heavy price in the form of more suffering.

This is not a time in history for any of us to be numb. One of the reasons it's so important that we become awake to our pain and to the pain of others is because in the absence of people whose concern is aroused by the problems of the world, those problems will only get much worse, not better. We can't afford to be numb to our own suffering or to the suffering of others.

Once, while browsing on the Internet, I saw the story of a bomb that had gone off that day at the end of an amateur soccer match in Iraq. Thirty-four people died in the ISIL bombing, seventeen of whom were between the ages of ten and sixteen. The article was accompanied by a heartbreaking picture of a young man comforting what appeared to be a teenage boy, the boy's face so shattered by the incident that had occurred at the closing of what has to be one of the few joys left to young people in his war-torn country.

I thought about the horror of that incident, and the horror of that war. Most horrible of all was the realization that none of it had to happen; that the chaos in Iraq today is the consequence of a terrible act perpetrated by the government of my own country. I was reminded of the bitter words spoken to me by a Baghdadi woman on a radio show I hosted a few years ago: "Before Saddam Hussein was killed, we knew we had three devils: him and his two sons. And we spent all our time planning what we would do when they died. But what your country has done, there are so many devils now that we cannot possibly deal with them all."

As awful as it felt for me to think about this—*as depressing as it was*—I would not wish to have been buffered from my pain that day. As Gandhi said, there is *soul force* in bearing witness to the agony of others. The least I can do is not buffer myself from my pain, when that young boy cannot buffer himself from his.

Numbing our sensitivity to the problems of the world not only diminishes our humanity, but also decreases our motivation to fix those problems before they overwhelm us. We don't need to avoid our suffering as much as we need to heed its message. The fabric of our civilization is dangerously frayed, and the people who understand that—who are genuinely and appropriately upset about it—are the passion-bearers needed to re-create the world.

Yet there is subtle disdain for such passion-bearers today. Some seem to think they're too cool to care. After a recent Hollywood Oscars ceremony, a popular television and movie actress expressed scorn for Oscar winners who used their platform to talk about the environment or corporate greed—the issues about which they were passionate. She said she was happy she lives in New York, where apparently such "Hollywood bullshit" does not occur! It was just too much for her. "Guys," she said, "pick a lane!" Later that week, I saw her starring in a television commercial for American Express. Yep! She picked her lane.

But those who are awake to what's happening on the planet today aren't looking for approval. They're looking for a better world, and without apology. Author Paul Hawken has coined the phrase "blessed unrest" to describe a general sense of unease that many people feel. If anything should be worrisome, it's how many people are *not* horrified by so much unnecessary suffering in the world today. Sometimes neurosis is best measured not by the things that make us sad, but by the things that do *not* make us sad.

Grief over the grievous state of the world is healthy; where would we be if abolitionists had not been upset about slavery, or suffragettes had not been upset that women could not vote? Such upset is an early warning inside our guts, saying, "The world is going in the wrong direction." People are depressed today because the world is devolving. *We are not wrong to feel this way.* Rather, we should be listening to the voice in all of us that's saying: "Something is wrong here. Something is wrong." Then we are awakened to the urgent call of history: that we must make it right.

Every problem emerges originally from a mindset, and every solution emerges from a mindset as well. The problem is not just that we have so many problems; the problem is that too many people feel numb to them, or powerless to fix them, or hopeless, or disillusioned. Disillusionment, however, can be a good thing when it motivates us to mature. Becoming stripped of the illusion that "someone else" will fix our problems, we become aware that we ourselves must do it. Once we're out there trying to make a difference, we start to feel that something different is possible.

The correct question is not, "Why do starvation, or genocide, or deep poverty exist?" The question is, "Why do we *allow* such things to exist?" The people who repudiate and stop such things share a common characteristic: *they refuse to shut up.* In the words of Martin Luther King Jr., "Our lives begin to end the day we become silent about things that matter."

When I was young, there were specific issues we could rail against—the Vietnam War, lack of civil rights, gender inequality— and we did. The problem today is that there is more than just one war over here or one oppressive institution over there; those, we could fix. Our problem now is vaguely all-encompassing, less limited to a particular effect and more an underlying blanket of cause. That overriding cause is the effective yet soulless mindset that's the child of the new corporatized order, threatening to marginalize anyone who doesn't play along with an increasingly destructive way of looking at the world.

The bottom line is money now—not people or principles or love. And that bottom line is apparently not to be questioned. Fear argues that we're not here to love each other and that we owe each other nothing. We're here to get more stuff, though whatever the stuff is rarely satiates our hunger. Once we get the stuff, we're supposed to be happy; and if we're not, then there must be something *wrong* with us. And there are many, many options for things we can do to assuage our existential pain. *Aren't we glad,* the ego asks, *to have so many choices?* But the truth is, our choices are expanded among consumer products while diminished among things that matter most. The ego is a stern emotional dictator, and there is to be no coloring outside the lines.

Yet where is the passion in always living inside the lines? Depression means something is depressed—as in our joy, our creativity, and sometimes, our ability to raise hell when hell needs to be raised. Depression is a lack of passion. Passion emerges when we've placed ourselves in service to that which is good, true, and beautiful—something important, something bigger than ourselves.

The passion-bearer's role is to recognize what's wrong in the world and invoke most passionately what could be made right. This role is not always easy, or smooth, or guaranteed to win universal applause. It's the heroic call of every age to smash old bottles and create new wine.

We can't put the wine of holiness inside a bottle of greed. We have financialized almost everything, disrupting the tender ecosystem of human relationships with a transactional mentality of "How can I get what I want from you?" that turns normal human encounters into sales calls. We are taught how to sell to one another—even to the point of gross manipulation and exploitation—more than we are taught how to love one another.

When "What do I want to get from you?" replaces "What am I here to share with you?"—when mutual beneficence and goodwill are no longer the basis of human relationships—the world begins to fall apart. Normal human interactions become skewed, and huge socioeconomic forces become unjust.

People in some of the richest nations in the world are among the most depressed, not because they lack material goods, but because they lack a sense of community. During the past few decades, we've sacrificed social elements essential to the cultivation of community, family, and inner peace at the altar of a new economic order.

The god of profit has overrun a God of righteousness as never before, with human suffering far too often viewed as acceptable collateral damage. Whatever it is, if it pays it stays—even when serious ethical concerns would argue that it should not. This is not just a call for correction; it's a call for spiritual and political revolution.

It is indeed a revolutionary act today to stand firm for compassionate principles in the face of an unfettered economic behemoth.

Righteous relationships with other human beings are essential to our peace and happiness, both among individuals and among nations, because we were not created as isolated creatures. We are interdependent by nature. We are born to be brothers and sisters, and in the absence of kinship we slowly die.

Thinking ourselves separate and alone within our isolated lives, we lose all sense of responsibility to each other, compassion for each other, and forgiveness of each other. This is the ego mind's death trap, both for individuals and for society; and the fact that we are very, very sad about it is one of the healthiest things that can be said about us. Without love we are without life, and deep in our hearts we know this.

NATURE'S EARLY
WARNING SYSTEM

I heard a story once about a chimpanzee troop in which a portion of the population displayed depressed behavior. They didn't eat with the rest of the chimps, play with the rest of the chimps, or sleep with the rest of the chimps. A group of anthropologists wondered what effect the absence of these depressed chimps would have on the rest of the troop and removed them for six months. When they returned, they found that all of the other chimps, those who remained in the troop, had died! Why? According to one analysis, the chimps perished because the so-called depressed chimps among them had been their early warning system. The depressed chimps had been depressed for a reason: they registered that a storm was coming, or snakes, or elephants, or disease. The presence of the depressed chimps had been an evolutionary aid to the survival of the entire population; in their absence, the other chimps did not notice the dangers that lurked.

Nothing could be more functional than an internal warning system, among people or among any other species. And nothing could be more *dys*functional than to ignore the warning or to *take the edge off*. And we do this in so many ways.

Our contemporary popular culture is itself a numbing agent, making us inappropriately comfortable when we should instead be appropriately uncomfortable. There is even an ersatz spirituality now cultivating the belief that since the world is an illusion anyway, why bother to try to fix things? What a convenient excuse for not helping. In fact, no serious spiritual path gives anyone a pass on addressing the suffering of other sentient beings. We're not here to ignore the darkness of the world, but to transform it. And in order to transform the darkness, we must at times engage it.

Martin Luther King Jr. didn't just urge people to love their oppressors; he also urged them to boycott the bus company. Outrage at social injustice is hardly a dysfunctional reaction to it; moral outrage is born not of anger, but of love. There is no mammalian species in which the fierce protectiveness of a mother toward her young is not requisite for the survival of that species. It's not negative to yell "Fire!" if indeed a house is burning; what's negative is to sit there and do nothing.

Only the ego believes we have no moral responsibility to address the pain of others, or that there will be no bitter consequences if we do not. But the Law of Cause and Effect is real; or, to put it another way, karma is a bitch. Of course it hurts to register the unnecessary suffering of others, but it will ultimately hurt much more if we deny it. A ribbon of love runs through our veins, like electric impulses connecting us to every other living thing. Acting out of accordance with this reality puts us out of our center and out of our joy. We give ourselves more emotional permission to party in the evening when we know we did all we could to be there for others during the day.

Many of us feel like we're aliens in this world—because spiritually, we are. And feeling spiritually homeless, of course we feel sad. But we're on the earth to make it our home, not to acquiesce to all the ways that it isn't that now. The manifestations of fear have become so potent—yes, within a realm of illusion, but within that illusion people suffer and die—that it is time for a great revolution of consciousness. It is time to claim the earth for the forces of love.

Nothing is a greater antidote to depression than to join love's revolution, taking even the tiniest step to contribute energy to the transformational wave of consciousness now rising up among us. This is not just a way to make a dent in the epidemic of depression; it is the way we will save the world.

We transform the world with every loving, forgiving thought. We transform it with every political, social, or economic act of resistance to a loveless order. We transform it with any act of creation that points to a new way of being on the planet. That transformation—both personally and societally—is the evolutionary next step for humanity.

We will take that step, or we will become extinct like any other species whose behavior becomes so maladaptive, so against the grain of its survival that it is literally cast off the earth. That is where we are headed now, and yet, we can choose another way. As with every other miracle, God shows His hand at the most amazing times, in the most mysterious ways. In the darkness of night there is a star of new hope, as there has always been and always shall be.

Dear God,

For me and all the world,

Please pave a path of light out of darkness

And show us how to walk it.

Open our eyes to see

And our minds to understand

Another way to be,

Another path to follow,

That we might live

Another way.

Dear God,

Please use us

To make the world a better place.

Amen

SIX

Forgiveness

While it's important not to gloss over our pain, it's equally important to keep the endgame in sight. And the endgame is happiness. As much as the mind is depressed when out of sync with its spiritual reality, it is happy when realigned with it. Happiness is not just the promised land of spiritual seeking; it is our natural state, the paradise from whence we came and to which all of us long to return.

Nothing is more joyful than an infant's laugh, and nothing is more beautiful than an infant's smile. And all of us were that infant at one time. We came to the earth with a propensity for joy, and lost it because of the lies we've been taught here. The ongoing problem is that we have internalized those lies, to a point where they are continuous mental habit patterns that deny us the joy of living.

According to *A Course in Miracles*, the purpose of our lives is to be happy. That is the same thing as saying that enlightenment, salvation, forgiveness, compassion—all the facets of a holy mind—are the keys to happiness. One of the most pernicious lies of the ego is that we must choose between being happy and serving God; in fact, in a very real way, the only way we CAN be happy is by serving God. For God is love, and without love we are bereft.

We do not learn spiritual principles in order to live lives of sacrifice, but in order to live lives of abundance and peace and joy. God does not deliver us from suffering so we can be kinda sorta sometimes okay; he delivers us from suffering so we can laugh like we did when we were children and thought we would never laugh that way again. Such is the glory and mighty power of God.

The question is not, then, what do we have to do in order to be happy? The question is who do we have to be in order to be happy? How do we have to think? How can we best love?

WHAT FORGIVENESS REALLY IS

Without forgiveness, there is no love; and without love, there are no miracles. It is written in *A Course in Miracles* that we can have a grievance or we can have a miracle, but we cannot have both. Forgiveness, therefore, is the most essential key to happiness. Sometimes the challenge is to forgive others, and sometimes the challenge is to forgive ourselves. But suffering remains until we forgive.

Ego views forgiveness very differently from the way spirit does. The ego posits that someone is guilty and then deigns to forgive that person as an act of spiritual superiority. Obviously, this is not really forgiveness as much as judgment posing as something else. True forgiveness is the recognition that because only love is real, whatever needs forgiving exists only within the realm of illusion. We release our focus on someone's guilt and instead embrace the knowledge of his or her eternal innocence. In doing so—by the power of this one mental shift in perception—we unleash the power of the miraculous universe.

Forgiveness resets the trajectory of probabilities that otherwise unfold wherever guilt and blame prevail. Where love is expressed, miracles occur naturally; where love is denied, miracles are deflected. Forgiveness frees miracles to intercede on behalf of our holiness and restore harmony where it had been blocked.

We seek to forgive not as a way of denying what has been done to us, but as a way of transforming our experience of what was done to us. As we shift our focus from the realm of the body to the realm of spirit, we move beyond our attachment to the thought of someone's guilt. No longer according reality to that person's transgression, the mind stops according reality to the pain it caused. This is not denial, but transcendence. It activates the self-correcting mechanism of the universe, altering the effects of any transgression against us. No one has the power to permanently defeat us as long as we are willing to forgive.

Forgiveness is a selective remembering of what someone did right, at a time when the ego mind is shrieking about what someone did wrong. We always have a choice about where to focus—whether to blame someone or to bless someone. I can concentrate my attention on what you did wrong, or I can seek to remember a moment when you tried to do right. Although the ego insists that you don't deserve it, the spirit absolutely knows that you do. And my ego has an ulterior motive: in seeking to attack you, it is seeking secretly to attack me. Only when I remember who you really are (*an innocent child of God, regardless of your mistakes*) can I remember who I really am (*an innocent child of God regardless of mine*).

A Course in Miracles says that whenever we're tempted to have an attack thought about another person, we should imagine a sword about to fall on their head—and then remember that because there's only one of us here, the sword is falling on our own head. An idea doesn't leave its source; therefore, whatever I think about you, I am thinking about myself. In attacking you, I am attacking myself. And in forgiving you, I am forgiving myself.

Condemning another person, then, while it might give us a few minutes of temporary relief, will always boomerang and make us feel worse. If I attack you, you will attack me back—or at least I'll think you did. In terms of how consciousness operates, it doesn't matter who attacked first: whoever attacks, feels attacked.

Forgiveness takes us off the wheel of suffering. It delivers us to quantum realms beyond time and space, where thoughts of guilt have marred neither your innocence nor mine. This is summed up in a line from the Persian poet Rumi: "Out beyond ideas of wrongdoing and rightdoing, there is a field. I'll meet you there." There, in that space of no-thing, the universe miraculously self-corrects. In the presence of love, things automatically return to divine right order. That which the ego has made imperfect is returned to the track of divine perfection, releasing possibilities for healing that would not otherwise exist.

"I'm sorry."

"I'm sorry too."

Simple words, and how much better those words are than the ego's alternative. How often we have said things very different than that, which then for years we regret having said.

Few things are more emotionally painful than unwarranted distance between ourselves and others. The ego creates the distance through judgment and attack. Forgiveness is when we then stand up to the ego, commanding it to go back to the nothingness from whence it came. We choose instead to think as God thinks, and God does not condemn. God does not condemn because He sees us only as He created us. We will be at peace, and the world will be at peace, when we learn to see each other as God does. Learning to do this is the only reason we're here.

THE HOLY INSTANT

The ego's perception of time is linear, but linear time is an illusion. The only real time is God's time, or eternity. The only place where eternity intersects linear time is in the present moment, called in *A Course in Miracles* the "Holy Instant." That is where miracles happen.

One of the daily lessons in the Workbook of *A Course in Miracles* is, "The past is over. It can touch me not." Since only love is real, only the love you were given and that which you gave others, was real in your past. Nothing else need be brought with you into the shining present. Leave behind what wasn't real to begin with, and every moment can be a new beginning.

The future is programmed in the present. If we enter the present carrying thoughts of the past, we program the future to be just like the past. But when we enter the present without the past, we free the future to be unlike it. Miracles occur in the present, interrupting the linear sequence of time. Forgiveness is what happens when we choose to see someone not as they were before this moment, but as who they are right now. Entering into the Holy Instant, free of our focus on what happened in the past, we free a relationship to begin again. I give you a break, increasing the probability that you'll give me one too.

God sees only our innocence because that is how He created us, and therefore only that is true. In training our minds to see people as He does, we allow miracles to heal our relationships and free us from our suffering over them. Only when we release someone from our condemnation of what they did do we free ourselves of the effects of what they did. By giving the gift of forgiveness, we receive the gift of forgiveness. It is not an act of sacrifice, but an act of self-interest.

Entering the Holy Instant, consciously focusing on the spiritual innocence that is the truth of someone's being *now*, in this moment, I re-mind that person of their innocence and thus re-mind myself of mine. In that one miraculous instant, the veil of illusion is removed and an entire universe of otherwise unmanifest possibilities flows forth.

The ego, of course, sees all of this as nonsense. Given that separation is its goal, it deems all efforts to forgive as offensive. It specializes in comments like, *"But you should be angry!"*; *"You'll just be a doormat if you forgive this"*; and *"I'm really worried about you; you seem to have no boundaries."*

But the ego is a liar. That which restores us to our right minds does not guide us incorrectly. The fact that I forgive you doesn't mean that I've lost my mind. It doesn't mean that I can't say no. It doesn't mean that I can't set healthy boundaries or leave unhealthy situations. If anything, it means that I can do so more quickly and effectively. Having been lifted above the emotional turmoil created by hurtful events, my ability to wisely navigate the material world is only improved. If it's wise to leave a situation, to say no, to turn away from someone—it will only increase my effectiveness if I can do so kindly.

Being able to nonreactively and simply leave a situation is far more powerful than stomping my feet and screaming, "No one is going to treat me this way!" For with the latter comes the inevitability of the fact that, yes, someone *will* treat you that way. For when we are angry, there is still a gap between our present personality and our enlightened self. The situation will reappear, with another person in another town perhaps, until we learn to close that gap. Who we have not forgiven remains in our head. As *A Course in Miracles* reminds us, the warden can't leave the prison any more than the prisoner can.

Forgiveness is a process, and it doesn't mean the person we forgive will necessarily be our friend—for a while, or ever. If you've done something awful to me or to someone I love, I don't see myself hanging out and having lunch with you anytime soon. If a woman lives with an abuser, she needs to leave the relationship. Forgiveness does not mean there are no boundaries, accountability, laws, or healthy standards of behavior. It means merely that there's a way for us to find peace in our hearts, regardless of someone else's behavior. And that itself is a miracle.

A young man I knew with AIDS once said to me, "You mean, I have to forgive *everybody?*" I remember laughing and saying to him,

"Well, I don't know. What do you have, the flu, or AIDS? Because if you only have the flu, just forgive a few people! Otherwise, you might want to consider taking all of the medicine."

If we think about all the people we have known, and the people we know now, it's usually amazing how many judgments we hold. Tremendous weight is lifted from our shoulders when we forgive and let them go.

Dear God,

I am willing to see my brother differently,

Despite what he might have done to me.

Release him from the sword of my condemnation

That I too might be released.

Show me his innocence

That we might both be free.

Fill my mind with the spirit of forgiveness.

Open my eyes that I might see

That only love is real.

May I see through this veil

To the light beyond,

That Your love might heal my heart.

Amen

FREEDOM FROM THE PAST

Clearly, there is evil in the world. Forgiveness is not a topic that underestimates the reality of evil, glibly advising us to pour pink paint over something terrible and pretend that it didn't happen. Love doesn't destroy our brain cells or lower our IQs. We can recognize that something bad happened but still see the futility of fury and the self-indulgence of outsized anger.

God does not need us to police the universe. Our anger, our bitterness, only deflects His miracles. The spiritual universe is self-correcting. Despite what anyone might have done to you in the past, God has a mysterious plan by which your future is programmed to be better. Nothing anyone did to you, but only your anger at them for having done so, can stop the miraculous flow of love to your door.

A Course in Miracles asks if we prefer to be right or to be happy. Forgiveness does not mean we're condoning something we think should not be condoned. It means only that we're freeing ourselves from the agony of its effects. We forgive the past in order to be free of it.

My friend Naomi Warren spent two years of her life, from ages twenty-one to twenty-three, in Auschwitz. She told me that upon her liberation, her thought was this: "Hitler got two years of my life. He will not get another day." The fact that someone who has experienced the horror of a Nazi concentration camp can not only survive but thrive proves the psyche's profound ability to heal itself. I have known others like Naomi—people who have experienced things that would make most of us buckle under the pain, from the murder of a child to heinous abuse during their own childhoods. All of them are beacons of possibility and an honor to know, embodying the miracle of God's specialty at bringing forth light from total darkness. They are demonstrations of a holy consciousness at work, inspirations to those of us whose own struggles to survive seem so small in comparison. If people who have suffered at the hands of genuine evil are able to move on in their lives, then surely those of us who suffer things far less onerous can find the strength to get on with ours.

FORGIVING OURSELVES

There are times in life when our greatest challenge is to forgive ourselves. *A Course in Miracles* says that we pay a very high price for refusing to take responsibility for our experience: the price of not being able to change it. The fact that it makes us *feel bad* to realize that we might have done wrong is simply the sign of a healthy personality. When people tell us, "You can't make a mistake," but we know we did, their advice, however well-intentioned, isn't helpful. It is important to own our mistakes in order to learn from them.

Perhaps we *did* screw up. Perhaps we *did* behave irresponsibly and recklessly. Perhaps we *did* do something egregious. We might realize that what went wrong in a situation was at least partly due to our own mistakes, and now we're suffering paroxysms of self-hatred. The ego is fine with that, because it doesn't really care who we're attacking as long as we're attacking someone. Its first response to our past errors is to refuse to own them, but if that doesn't work, it turns to self-flagellation. The ego is that which both leads us to do the wrong thing and then punishes us savagely for having done so.

The important thing to do when we know in our hearts that we've been wrong is to look open-eyed, even if teary-eyed, at exactly what we did and why we did it. It's very important to own our mistakes if indeed we made them. We may end up with a painful conscience, but that's appropriate, for only a sociopath has no remorse. Minimizing our regret, numbing the pain of conscience, dulling our own lamentation is not the way to enlightenment. This is one of the areas in life where only burning through the pain will get us to the gain. Grownups own up to our mistakes, and grow from them.

And when we do take an honest look at the darkness in our hearts, we might be surprised at what we see there. We find that our mistakes, our character defects, are simply the coping mechanisms of the frightened child who still lives within us. We had to have been very hurt in life to have concocted such a dysfunctional way of dealing with things. Behind the blackened heart is a fragile heart—in all of us.

God would have us look on ourselves, and on each other, as He does. God is love, and He created us in his image. An angry God is the ego's fiction, created in *its* image. This does not, however, change who God really is or how He really works. Our mistakes are met not by His wrath, but by His mercy.

God would have us show to ourselves, and to each other, the mercy He shows to us. It is as blasphemous to attack ourselves as it is to attack others. In any moment when we made a mistake, when we downloaded into the world a version of ourselves that is at odds with who we really are, then we did not uncreate who we really are; we simply chose not to express it. And we would have done differently had some wires not gotten crossed in our brains, had we felt that we could show our love in that moment and still get our needs met. When I have made my worst mistakes, I didn't wake up in the morning and say, "I think I'll be a jerk today!" Rather, in my mistaken moments, I got deeply, insanely, terrifyingly confused, as did anyone else who ever acted out of fear.

Having made a mistake, we should feel appropriate remorse, yes—but not gorge on feelings of guilt and self-condemnation. God calls us not to punish ourselves, but to atone for our errors and go forward on higher ground. Only the ego would have us tarry in the fields of self-hatred. The only antidote to self-hatred is self-respect, and self-respect can come only when we know we're doing everything possible to be better people now.

All of us have done things we regret and lived through situations that make us cringe when we remember them. The ego's response to past error is psychological imprisonment through emotional self-punishment. God's response is psychological liberation through the power of the Atonement.

The Atonement is the correction of our perceptions. It is one of God's greatest gifts. Expressed in the Catholic practice of confession, the Jewish Day of Atonement or Yom Kippur, and Alcoholics Anonymous through the taking of a fearless moral inventory and the making of amends, the Atonement principle is the cosmic reset button through which we are released from the otherwise negative consequences of wrong-minded action. Once we have atoned for a mistake, it no longer creates karmic consequences.

God sees our deviations from love not as sins to be punished but as errors to be corrected. As it says in *A Course in Miracles,* "All our sins are washed away by realizing they were but mistakes."

Dear God,

I know that I did wrong.

I place this situation in Your hands

And look clearly at the things I did,

Or the things I did not do,

By which I deviated from love.

Having made a wrong decision,

I make a different decision now.

Dear God, please correct my path.

Remove from me my feelings of guilt,

And make me a better person.

May I be ever more devoted

To doing what is right.

Release others from the consequences of

Any mistakes that I have made,

And please release me too.

Amen

MERCY, MERCY

Imagine your life as a computer. A permanent, undeletable file is available called "God's Will," literally meaning "Love's Thought." The file is always there, available for download. The only question is whether or not we choose to download it.

Obviously, ours is a world where the file of infinite, unconditional love is not downloaded nearly enough. Too often we download the energy of our broken, tortured, frightened selves, manifesting the subtle and not-so-subtle violence in our hearts—hence the consciousness of the human race and the state of the world in which we live.

But even though love can be unchosen, it cannot be uncreated. When any of us expresses fear instead of love, the love we *could* have expressed remains safely ensconced in the Mind of God. According to *A Course in Miracles*, whatever miracle we've deflected is held in trust for us until we are ready to receive it. The Atonement allows us to reclaim whatever good we might have denied ourselves. Situations will come around again, returning to us "the years that the locusts have eaten."

What the ego steals, God gives back.

Seeing how opportunities reemerge after we have genuinely atoned, we glimpse God's mercy. "Mercy" is a word that means very little until we have actually felt it. And once we do, we are changed forever. We are in awe of the way the universe rearranges itself to give us yet another chance.

The concept of religious sanctuary is an old one: no matter what crime someone had committed, if that person made it into a church, or other sanctuary zone, and claimed "Mercy," then they could not be arrested for a crime. It was believed that in that moment, they aligned themselves with God's power such that all judgment upon them was nullified. While few today would see this as a reasonable practice for law enforcement, the spiritual principle involved has profound relevance to personal relationships.

God is not under the impression that we never make mistakes. Given the fact that the thinking of the world is so deeply insane, it's almost surprising that we don't make bigger mistakes more often! And it is only the ego's arrogance that might have ever tempted us to believe we were incapable of error. All of us are growing, and all of us stumble at times. Anything can become a platform for a miracle, and sometimes the fact that we *do* stumble makes us better people afterward. Among other things, feeling God's mercy on us increases our mercifulness toward others. Having experienced mercy, we become better at mercy. For instance, I've caught myself about to judge a young woman for irresponsibly throwing around her sexual energy, and then reminded myself, "Uh, Marianne, she's *nothing* compared with what *you* were like!"

God's love for us does not waver. He loves each of us as He loves all of us: not because of what we've done or not done, but because of who we are. He knows who you are because He created you, and God's creation cannot be changed. He knows that your mistakes occurred only within the realm of illusion. He is ready to begin again whenever you are.

Earlier in my life, I would atone for mistakes easily enough but then too often stray back into the same mistaken behavior. And then I'd start the process all over again. After repeated cycles of mess-up-your-life-then-fall-to-your-knees, mess-up-your-life-then-fall-to-your-knees, one day I finally said to myself, "Next time you're down on your knees, Marianne, just stay there!"

Sometimes, it's having made enough mistakes that then inspires us to live differently. The Atonement becomes more than just something that helped to ease our pain; once our hearts are acquainted with its power, trying to live it becomes a consistent way of life.

Forgiveness is ultimately not just an act, but an attitude; not a relationship tool, but a state of mind. And it is not just an attitude toward people, but toward life itself. Forgiveness is the ultimate correction of perception that dissolves all the darkness of the world. It is a tincture of pure, unadulterated light.

FORGIVENESS AS THE WAY

The veil that separates this world from the celestial order is like gossamer silk with the strength of titanium. On one hand, it is simply a thought; but on the other hand, every thought is powerful. Thoughts of guilt and fear are a living hell from which forgiveness and love deliver us.

From losing a job unfairly to losing a relationship, from being betrayed to being victimized, from feeling abandoned to feeling oppressed—events are transformed, and the suffering they cause us is assuaged, as we learn to forgive them. Forgiveness isn't always easy—sometimes it's a process—but it is never without its rewards.

Some might argue that reinterpreting life through the eyes of love is simply looking at it through rose-colored glasses. Yet the "observer effect" in science posits that when the perceiver changes, so does that which is perceived. If someone tells you that you're being an overly optimistic Pollyanna, just thank them for the compliment. For Pollyanna is the story of a miracle-worker. She did not just *see* the love in people despite their loveless behavior; through her seeing she *invoked* their love, and their behavior ultimately changed.

The ego keeps us bound to the illusion that we exist entirely subject to the material world, when in fact the world is nothing but the projection of our thoughts. Beyond this world there is a truer one; as we extend our perceptions beyond what our physical senses perceive to what we know to be true in our hearts, we are delivered to the world that lies beyond. As we extend our perceptions beyond the veil of physicality, we experience the miracle of deliverance from all the suffering of the world.

Within the three dimensions of our worldly experience, this or that circumstance did or does exist. But how we choose to look at the circumstance will determine how it ultimately affects us. To forgive is to remember that only love is real and nothing else exists, and what does not exist cannot defeat you. In every moment we forgive, we remember this. In every moment we forgive, we awaken from our suffering. In every moment we forgive, another tear begins to dry.

Dear God,

I give to You my pain and despair.

I know that I suffer

Because I see what is not there.

I know that I cry

Because my faith in You is weak.

Please open my mind

That I might know,

And open my eyes

That I might see.

Bring comfort to my soul, dear God,

And forgiveness to my heart.

Amen

SEVEN

Relationship Heaven, Relationship Hell

The pain of relationship difficulties—both while we're in them and when we're losing them—can be excruciating. Here, as with everything else, an understanding of spiritual reality is key to attaining a peaceful heart.

When we think with love, we are being ourselves. The mind when it is wholly loving is whole, or holy. That is the source of happiness.

When we hold a grievance against someone, however, we are using our minds noncreatively, or destructively. This splits the mind in two and puts us at war against ourselves. That is the source of mental anguish.

Taking responsibility for the nature of our thinking is thus our greatest power to heal our lives. The dominant thought system of the world constantly tempts us to attack others, thereby attacking ourselves. But when we give our minds to God to use for His purposes, they become holy touchstones of another way of thinking and being. Our purpose on the earth is to see every moment as an opportunity to love. We thus become miracle-workers, or transformers of darkness into light.

Every moment of every day, whether someone is in a room with us or we're just thinking about them, we're faced with the decision: Will I bless this person, or will I judge them? It is quite astonishing to bear witness to what we're actually thinking. Of the many thousands of thoughts that we think each day, most of them take issue on some level with what someone did or does. Whether it's something seemingly innocuous, such as "She should have put that glass in the dishwasher," or something truly negative, such as "I hate that bastard," a grievance is a grievance. According to *A Course in Miracles*, any grievance we hold against anyone for any reason is an attack upon ourselves.

You can't stop the war against yourself by ending only some of the battles. In taking up a spiritual path, we seek a loving attitude toward all—not just some. None of this has to do with how we "should" think or "should" be; it simply has to do with understanding the power of every thought.

We're often deluded by the myth of neutrality—the idea that if we don't actively wish anyone harm, then that is enough. But in fact there are no neutral thoughts. Our thinking can be mismanaged, but its power cannot be diminished; every single thought is a cause that will lead to an effect.

Sometimes I'll be rushing through an airport with all the other travelers to this or that gate, to reach a plane that will take me to yet another city, to repeat the same pattern of speaking and book signing, and then return home exhausted. If my mind is attuned only to that physical reality, then I can feel overwhelmed and depleted.

Or, I can choose again. "Snap out of it, Marianne," I'll say to myself. And then, instead of closing myself off in an effort to protect myself from the mental jangle around me, I'll look around at the people in the airport and send them my love. I will think about who they are, where they're going, how many of them might be enduring hardships in their lives. How many of them might be ill or grieving. How many of them might be stressed about finances, or their marriages, or their children. How most of them are good, noble people, trying their best to live decent lives. When I do this, the greatest medicine—compassion—begins to flood my heart. My experience of my experience changes. What my ego had interpreted as "just another airport" becomes a holy temple where I have the extraordinary privilege of trying to love as God loves. My heart, my mind, even my body rise above the ego as I remember the truth of who I am by remembering the truth of who others are. A contented smile replaces a stressed-out frown.

The problem is not that doing this is difficult so much as it's *different*. Training ourselves to use our minds as vessels of love runs against the grain of our usual mental habits. Yet it is the only true deliverance from the sorrow in our hearts.

Someone might say, "All that's wonderful, Marianne, but right now I've got bigger issues to deal with than going around blessing strangers." And we all do. But one of the problems with sadness, depression, and anxiety is that they tempt us to isolate ourselves—if not physically, then at least mentally and emotionally. Yet no matter how much pain we're in, we can choose to love others. No matter how many tears we might have cried today, we can still look out upon someone else with an open heart. In truth, they probably cried as many tears as we have. In our compassion for what others have been through, the universe pours forth its compassion on us. We never really know what lies in the hearts of other people, but once we consider that everyone else is as sensitive as we are, and everyone else has hurt as much as we have, then our hearts are flooded with divine light and no darkness can hold us back. No matter what our pain or heartbreak, as long as we keep our hearts open to others, then new life will spring up around us.

None of this is merely a matter of theory; it's only meaningful if borne out by practical experience. And it will be. Next time you're waiting in a line at a store or sitting in a restaurant, silently send peace and love from your heart to the people near you. Your energy, the look on your face, even what you say and how you say it will change. And see whether or not what you put out then comes back to you. You might be reading a book like this one, but the words in a book can't substitute for the power of your decision to see another person as a child of God. The only church, the only temple, the only shrine that ultimately matters is the ground on which you stand right now. It might be an airport. It might be a deli. It might be your bedroom. Just make it holy, and peace will come.

RELATIONSHIP ASSIGNMENTS

According to *A Course in Miracles*, relationships are spiritual assignments in which the Holy Spirit brings together those who have the maximal opportunity for soul growth. It should be no surprise to us, then, that relationships are not always easy. They're magnifying glasses through which we can view what does and does not work in how we're relating to other people. Every situation in life is a relationship in which we—and often those around us—can see exactly where we are free to love, and where we are bound by fear.

While the ego would argue that there's a different kind of love for different kinds of relationship, the spiritual basics of relationship are the same no matter what form a relationship takes. Whether you're my business acquaintance or a family member, the issue is this: Am I meeting you on the level of my personality, or am I extending to you the gift of my love? Am I here to judge you, or to forgive you? The answers will determine what happens next.

The ego sees other people from a transactional perspective, looking for how others can serve our needs. The spirit sees other people from a relational perspective, seeking for ways that together we can serve love. To the ego, relationships are fear-laden traps; to the spirit, they are holy encounters. The last thing the ego wants us to believe is that relationships form the basis of the spiritual journey. But they do. Every encounter, large or small, is an opportunity to glorify love. When I surrender a relationship to serving God's purpose, the relationship most probably will bring me peace. If I try to use it to serve my needs as I define them, then it most probably will bring me pain.

So how do we get our needs met if our only purpose is to love? How do we set standards, get work done, have reasonable expectations, and not get taken advantage of if we see ourselves in any situation only as a miracle-worker, a channel for love, a servant of God?

The answer is, "Far more easily." The miracle does not occur on the bodily level; it has less to do with what happens on the outside than with what happens on the inside. People can feel when they're being blessed, and they can feel when they're being judged. Everyone subconsciously knows everything.

If I wake up in the morning and pray for your happiness, meditate on our spiritual oneness, set my intention on being a representative of love in your life today, surrender all temptation to control you or judge you, then you will *feel* that. Our relationship will have a chance at being a positive experience. Otherwise, it will be everything the ego wants it to be, and you will feel that too.

The primary issue in our relationship to anything is *purpose*. The ego's purpose in a relationship is to withhold love, while the spirit's purpose is to extend it. The ego sees the world as something to serve it, while the spirit sees the world as something for us to serve.

How many times have you been asked, "What are you looking for in a relationship?" rather than, "What is the greatest gift you feel you can bring to a relationship?" How many times has someone asked you in reference to a relationship, "Are you really getting what you need?" as opposed to, "Are you really giving all you have?" *A Course in Miracles* says that the only thing lacking in any situation is what we're not giving. It's amazing how often we're counting up someone else's demerits, while hardly giving any attention to our own. The wily, insidious ego calls this self-care.

The ego sees every relationship as a chance to monitor another person's spiritual progress, but never our own. The ego is like a scavenger dog seeking any possible evidence of another's guilt, that we might attack, judge, criticize, and blame him or her. Its ultimate purpose is not to hurt the other, however, as much as it is to hurt us.

The ego never sees a reason to be satisfied with someone. It slyly tempts us to the thoughts and behavior that would keep love at bay, even while protesting that we want it desperately. "The only reason I want you to be different is because I *love* you!" According to *A Course in Miracles,* the ego's dictate is "seek, but do not find."

In a world where fear dominates the consciousness of the human race, it takes conscious practice to develop the emotional musculature of love. But boy is this hard when someone pushes all our buttons and triggers all our wounds. We can be all lovely and enlightened in the morning, and crazed with anger by noon.

And then, unfortunately, we're off to the races. Some of the biggest judgments we make, the most pernicious attacks, are made before we even have a chance to think. We send a reactive text or email. We say things we later regret having said. We make decisions that only in retrospect we see as having been self-sabotaging.

This is why spiritual practice is so important. The most powerful tool for success in life, in any area, including relationships, is that our minds be channels for right thinking. And for this, they must be trained.

We do weight-bearing exercises to train our physical muscles, and spiritual exercises to train our attitudinal muscles. The first give us the power to physically move, and the second give us the power to remain internally still. One empowers us externally, and one empowers us internally. And both take effort.

It's extremely helpful to spend time each morning, even if only five minutes, using whatever meditation or prayer technique you relate to, to train your attitudinal muscles to think with love. At the beginning of each day, before you meet or interact with anyone, consciously and proactively send your love before you. Then, say to yourself silently as you look at others throughout the day, "The love in me salutes the love in you." To any situation, surrender to God whatever judgments you bring with you. This kind of practice will give you more than peace; it will work miracles in your life. There's no room for darkness in a house that is filled with light, and there's no room for fear in a mind that is filled with love. The key to attracting, maintaining, and healing relationships is to fill our minds with light—surrendering ourselves to be used by God, that we might become a blessing on everyone we meet.

Consider affirming these truths each day:

1. I don't need anyone else to make me whole; as a creation of God, I am whole already. *I go into the world today to share with everyone I meet the abundant truth of who I really am.*

2. My function on the earth is to love, to forgive, and to bless. *Every person I will meet today is an opportunity for me to act as love's representative on earth.*

3. What I give to others, I give to myself. What I withhold from others, I withhold from myself. *Everyone I meet today provides me with an opportunity to increase my joy by bringing greater joy to others.*

As it says in *A Course in Miracles*, "prayer is the medium of miracles." Consider it one of the greatest powers in the miracle-worker's tool kit.

Dear God,

Please make my life

A sacred place

Not only for me,

But for those I meet.

May everyone who enters my life

Be blessed,

And may I be blessed by them.

Send to me those

With whom I am meant to grow.

Show us how to love each other

In ways that serve You best.

Amen

ATTRACTING LOVE

The universe itself is intentional, guiding all things to the actualization of their highest potential. This includes not only individuals, but also relationships. Love is always seeking us. The problem is how often we hide from it, scurrying away from the light of love into the darkness of our fearful selves. It wasn't that love didn't show up for us; it's that we didn't show up for love.

A Course in Miracles says that our job is not to seek love, but to seek all the barriers we hold against its coming. Those barriers, those walls in front of our hearts, are the places where we turn our backs on love. We do various things to keep love at bay, from behavior ranging from needy to controlling, dishonest to manipulative, avoidant to addictive, too hot to too cold, self-centered to smothering. These character defects are not where we're bad, but where we're wounded. Still, no matter what childhood experience might have caused those defects to begin with, they're our responsibility now. When we are displaying our rough edges, other people don't think, "Oh poor dear, you're wounded." They're more apt to think, "Oh Lord, get me out of here." Which totally makes sense.

So, time and time again, we find ourselves blowing it at relationships—with friends, with colleagues, with family, with partners. And once again, the only real problem is our separation from God. The key to fostering soulful relationships with others is fostering our primary relationship with God, for there, we're healed of the pieces of false self with which we so often sabotage our relationships.

In my relationship with God lies my relationship with my true self, and only when I'm aligned with the truth of who I am can I align with the truth in you.

HOSPITALS OF THE SOUL

Relationships are where we come to heal, not because we're always able to be our best within them, but precisely because we're not. They do not just highlight our strengths; they put a magnifying glass on our weaknesses. And in a way, that is their purpose. They do not just expose our rough edges; they give us the chance to smooth those edges out. Healing is a kind of detox process, in which everything that needs to leave our systems must first come up and then out. That which lies unhealed within us comes up for review, that we might consciously see where we're wounded in love and surrender the wound to God.

All of us are lonely, lonelier than we know, because we feel separate from God. And the ego, which is what convinces us that we're separate from Him to begin with, offers us the most twisted of solutions: that we find one special person who will complete us, and then we will not feel lonely. This is seeking salvation in separation, which will only deepen our despair.

The obsession with finding what in *A Course in Miracles* is called "a special relationship" is one of the biggest guns in the ego's arsenal. The reason we obsess about romantic love is because we project the expectation that it can heal the pain of our disconnectedness from the whole. We feel disconnected from God, from ourselves, from the earth, from other living beings; then, feeling bereft, we look for that one relationship that will make all the pain go away.

Wow, no *pressure* or anything.

Yet the idea of one special, exclusive relationship is a search for unity in separation. This goal of finding wholeness in one person not only counters the principle of enlightenment, it counters intimacy. For how could we be more intimate than that we *are* each other? Intimacy isn't something to try to create; it's something to accept as already accomplished. When we realize the other *is* us—not outside us—then we are likely to treat them as tenderly and as authentically as we would like to be treated. Which then creates . . . *intimacy!*

My ego decides I need *you* to behave a certain way in order to make *my* world okay. What I really need is to release you from the hook of my ego's agenda for your life! We can release our grip on other people's emotions, thoughts, and feelings. We can desist from writing agendas for other people's lives. And we can detach from thinking that anyone or anything external to ourselves is the source of our good.

When surrendered to God to use for His purposes, the ego's *special relationship* is transformed into a holy one. What *A Course in Miracles* calls a *holy relationship* is a hospital for the soul, where we recognize that our weaknesses will be made evident in the relationship for a reason.

If I only meet people who bring out my best, then, as wonderful as that is, there are probably some lessons left unlearned. It's in those places where our unconscious wounds are made conscious that we have the opportunity to heal them, because only then can we *see* them. Until then, they direct our lives in detrimental ways.

The closer we are to genuine joining, the greater the probability that the weaknesses of one partner or the other—usually both—will be subconsciously triggered. "You're needy and emotionally demanding" will meet "You're arrogant and selfish." Although the ego seeks relationship as a place to hide our wounds, the Holy Spirit uses relationships to bring those wounds to the surface—not to destroy the relationship, but to make it all that it can be. In the presence of mutual understanding, compassion, faith, and forgiveness, our wounds can be healed.

Sometimes, two people understand this, turning their relationship into a holy encounter and a conduit for continuous growth. Realizing that wounds are exposed in the relationship in order to be healed, they cleave to love despite resistance and commit to the effort of forgiveness and understanding.

She listens, and understands that her behavior was needy and controlling; she apologizes and behaves differently. He listens, and understands that his behavior was selfish and inconsiderate; he apologizes and behaves differently. As both become more aware of their own weaknesses—as they apologize, forgive, practice mercy, and seek to do better—the spiritual purpose of the relationship is served. Things that the ego sees as reasons to leave a relationship end up being things that the spirit sees as reasons why the relationship was formed. Sometimes, the lesson in a relationship is to stay and learn from what's happening, whereas at other times the lesson is to realize that it doesn't serve to remain there longer. There is no outer indicator of which lesson we are to learn; as with everything, the voice for God within us is ultimately the only reliable guidance system.

Whether the ultimate wisdom is to stay or to go doesn't matter as much as whether we use the experience to expand our hearts. Even if we're led to leave a relationship, it is as important that we be loving while leaving as that we be loving while staying. If we do not do this, then we will simply meet someone down the road who provides us with another opportunity to see our resistances to love, and to heal them.

TENDING THE GARDEN

Most of us are clear that once we buy a car, even if it's the best car in the world, we're going to have to do some things to maintain it. But for some mysterious reason, we often fail to recognize that we have to maintain our relationships just like that car. Anyone in his or her right mind sees a deep relationship with another human being as more precious than a *car*, but it's amazing how much more attention people will give to tending their "things" than to tending their relationships.

The most powerful way to tend a relationship is to place it in the hands of God each day. Surrender to God is not just a principle; it is something we *do*. At times I've said to people, "Did you pray about this?" and they have responded, "I know it's in God's hands." But that wasn't what I asked! I did not ask whether it was in God's hands (ultimately all things are); I asked whether they *put* it in God's hands. All things will ultimately result in a loving outcome, but it is completely up to us how long that will take. Through prayer, we invite the Holy Spirit to enter into our minds and readjust our thinking, to produce a loving outcome not just in an ultimate realm but in the reality of our daily lives right now.

Dear God,

May I be only a blessing on this person,

And may he be only a blessing on me.

Heal us in our wounded places

And cast out our resistances to love.

Lift our relationship to divine right order,

Above and beyond all walls that divide us.

May forgiveness purify

Our hearts and minds,

That we might see only the innocence

In ourselves and in each other.

May my presence in his life

Contribute to his happiness,

And serve him on his path.

May our joining be a holy thing.

May it serve Your purposes
For us and all the world
And bring joy to all living things.

Amen

None of us is perfect. All of us make mistakes. And close relationships are a place where we're bound to make them. In fact,
until we have seen someone's darkness, we don't really know them.
And until we've forgiven them their darkness, we don't really know
what love is.

Our relationships are temples of healing when we allow them
to be. The ultimate truth of any relationship is that two innocent
children of God are seeking to love and be loved. Someone else's
mistakes are simply where they hit walls which in that moment they
could not see beyond—and it's the same for us. *A Course in Miracles*
says that we should interpret all that is not love as a call for love. If
I judge you for your errors, I simply fortify them in your mind and
in mine. If I forgive your errors, I give both of us the chance to feel
the healing power of love.

Who among us is not scarred from the battles of love? Who
among us is not pained by the struggles of love? Who among us
is not longing for the comfort of love? As much as we all desire to
love and to be loved, in this wounded world it can be very hard at

times. But the only failure in love is to give up on love. A broken heart need not be a bitter heart. And while love can pause, it can never really end.

WHEN RELATIONSHIPS
CHANGE FORM

Relationships at their deepest level are not of the body, but of the spirit, and in that sense they are never over.

The crux of a relationship lies not in its form, but in its content, and change in form does not mean the end to a relationship at all. Even when we separate from someone, we are only appearing to do so because relationships are of the mind.

A couple who divorces, for instance, does not "end" a relationship, but merely changes its form. Understanding this perspective can make a huge emotional difference to a person who is having a hard time giving up attachment to the previous form of a relationship. When someone has left a relationship that we would have preferred to continue, or when someone has passed from this world and we're grieving their loss, the pain we feel can be crushing. But understanding the eternal nature of relationships—and the eternal nature of love—brings peace to even a tormented heart.

Sometimes we feel abandoned, betrayed, victimized, and heartbroken when a relationship changes form. But love to your door only stops if you stop it. That is why praying for the happiness of the lost lover is the surest way to transform your feelings. There is great emotional power in repeating about an estranged mate, over and over, "May he be blessed. May he be happy. May he be loved."

Some might say, "But how can I pray for his happiness? I hate him right now!" But blaming the other person for "abandoning" us, or refusing to respect his or her choice to move in another direction, is an attack on ourselves as much as an attack on them. It deflects the miracle we need right then. Such thinking, and the behavior it gives rise to, will only repel them and create more distance. And even more importantly, it will make it harder for us to move on; our hearts will be cramped in bitterness rather than be open to new love. When we ground ourselves in the realization that such a relationship is only changing form, we find ourselves able to release others to do what they need to do and to be where they need to be. Depending on our own mental choices, we can be a victim or a victor in love.

Dear God,

Please heal my shattered heart.

May I see only what is truly there

And not be tempted to judge my brother.

Despite my tears,

I pray that he be happy.

I bless him on his path

Though it has led him away from me.

Purify my mind of all thoughts of guilt

That we might both be free.

Create a path of light

For both of us.

Dissolve the cords that no longer serve,

And strengthen ones that do.

Bless my brother in all he does,

And please, dear God,

Bless me.

Amen

LOSING PEOPLE, LOSING THINGS

According to *A Course in Miracles*, everything is a relationship. Sometimes our relationship is with another person, but sometimes it's with a thing, a place, or even a dream we've cherished. Those relationships too can crash and burn.

I've known people who lost their entire life savings in an economic meltdown; soldiers who lost their limbs in war; people who lost their eyesight, their tongues, the use of their hands and feet due to disease; and people who survived years of abuse. I've known people so crumpled over from loss that they could hardly breathe. Yet

I've also known people who rose above such things and survived to live a happy life.

We're human beings, of course, so it's impossible to live our lives completely detached from the things of the world. But what we think while in the midst of darkness determines how quickly the light will come. When we are suffering through the pain of loss, miracles emerge when we realize that despite appearances, loss is an illusion. In God's universe there is no loss.

Only form can change, and only form can disappear. Content is changeless. The cycles of life and death are endless. What is yours is yours forever, and who is yours is yours forever. The universe is programmed for your happiness and automatically compensates in the realm of spiritual substance for any diminishment on the material plane. In a self-organizing, self-correcting universe, celestial forces immediately respond to all loss. For who you are cannot be diminished, and neither can your world. Not really. The changing miasma of the mortal world is merely an illusion, but you are not.

WHEN A LOVED ONE DIES

Because the ego posits that the life of the body is the only life, we interpret the death of the body as life's end. We are crushed when someone whom we loved has died, thinking that our relationship with him or her is over. I remember when my mother died, thinking I hadn't realized sadness could be so deep.

Having lost both my parents, my sister, and a best friend of thirty years, I've cried many tears over the death of loved ones. I've sat with parents who had to decide when to take their children off life support. I've grieved with young people who knew that the disease destroying them would kill them before the age of thirty. I've officiated at memorials of people who were murdered, and sat with their families while the horror set in. I am familiar with the reality of grief, both in my own life and in bearing witness to the agony of others.

According to *A Course in Miracles* and many other spiritual philosophies, life does not end with the death of the physical body. Birth of the physical body is not a beginning but a continuation, and the death of the physical body is not an end but a continuation. In an ultimate sense, death does not exist because those who live in the Mind of God live forever. The body is like a suit of clothes that we simply take off when it's no longer needed.

Faith does not keep us from grieving our lost loved ones, but it takes away the barbed wire otherwise wrapped around our hearts as we do. We can miss someone terribly yet be comforted by the realization that they're alive on another plane of existence. When I think of the family in which I grew up, I don't think of my father and my mother and my sister as gone, with only my brother and myself remaining. Rather, I see in my mind a photograph in which the three of them show in the negative and the images of Peter and me are exposed. But all five of us are still there.

Death does not end our relationships with those who passed. Life is a book without end; a single physical incarnation is simply one chapter of the book. In the next chapter, just as real, one person remains incarnate while the other lives on in invisible realms. Whom God hath brought together, no one and nothing—not even death itself—can put asunder.

In fact, amid grief, relationships can even improve. Forgiveness becomes easier when old hurts are seen in retrospect to have been unimportant. There is a way in which we see people more clearly once they've passed, and perhaps they see us more clearly, too.

When I think of my parents now, I am so much clearer about the gifts they gave me and so uninterested in the minor neuroses that mark the life of any family. I can rejoice that neither of them struggles with the challenges of sickness or old age any longer. Having felt at the time of my mother's death as though my umbilical cord had been turned backward and I wasn't sure that I even existed anymore, I now feel her invisible presence as a constant blessing in my life.

If I'm sad because I lost someone but feel deep inside that someday I will see that person again—that they are just in another room, in another dimension somewhere, still broadcasting although my set doesn't pick up their station—then I can move past my suffering more easily. I can find peace in something that is more than a memory—that is a living reality in my heart. If, on the other hand, I think death is a finite end, past which there is no further life of any kind, then a loved one's death remains a burden on my heart. Once again, the depth of my suffering depends to a large degree on how I interpret the experience.

I have come to trust the process of grief in my life and in the lives of others I've known. Suppressed tears are more dangerous than those that fall. Tears we cry can heal us, and tears we don't cry can hurt us. Among other things, denying ourselves permission to feel our sadness can desensitize us to the pain of others. And that is never a good thing. A period of mourning—with all its wailing, its tears, and its suffering—isn't necessarily the sign of a problem. It's simply the sign of love.

No one escapes permanently the experience of our death, and few of us escape the experience of mourning someone we love. These things are part of life. In older societies, death was more familiar because it was all around us. While of course we celebrate the fact that modern medicine has extended the average life span, we've paid a heavy price for pushing death to the periphery of our lives the way we have. Pushing it out of our homes, or even out of our minds, is not the answer—particularly as we age. In fact, in the words of Swiss psychologist Carl Jung, "Shrinking away from [death] is something unhealthy and abnormal which robs the second half of life of its purpose." We suffer more from death because we misinterpret it than because it exists. It is our fear and misunderstanding of death that causes most of our suffering—not death itself.

Dear God,

I place in Your hands the tears I cry

Over the death of my beloved.

May she rest forever in Your arms

And be at peace in her eternal home.

Send Your angels to comfort me as well,

That my eyes might be opened

To the nonreality of death.

Connect me, God, by a golden cord,

To the heart of my beloved.

For I would know that in Your love

She and I are one forever.

Amen

For some, the heartbreak is over our own impending death. It is a task of maturity to surrender into the knowledge that we too one day will die, relaxing into the eternal knowing that when we leave this life we do not really leave so much as expand into the cosmic space of All That Is. *A Course in Miracles* says that one day we will realize that death is not a punishment, but a reward. It says we will one day evolve to the point where physical death will not cause anyone sorrow. For we will know that in reality, there is no death.

For those who feel in their hearts that their time may be near, a prayer for comfort and peace—

Dear God,

Please take away my fear of death.

The pain in my heart, I surrender to You.

Please take away my suffering

And the suffering of those I love.

Open my eyes that I might see

The light beyond the veil.

Show me the truth of eternal life

That I might fear no more.

Take care of those

I leave behind.

Bring comfort to them and comfort to me.

Death has my heart so frightened now.

Please deliver me to peace.

Amen

EIGHT

Changing Ourselves, Changing the World

Many years ago during a period of time when I was deeply depressed, I often felt a strange presence, like someone sitting on the edge of my bed in the wee hours of the morning. This presence was a tall, thin shade sitting erect and very still, facing in a direction perpendicular to my body. I knew he wasn't a physical being, but I knew he was there. And I knew who he was.

I cannot describe what it meant to me that he was present. He never said any words or gave me any message. He was simply there. And I felt him around, not just at night. Although I sensed his actual presence at the end of my bed at night, during the day I simply felt him keeping watch.

Depressed and lonely, I was such a mess in those days. I knew I had turned into a rather pathetic person. I realized people looked at me with pity, thinking, "Too bad about Marianne." My cousin told me years later that during that time, my father said to her with tears in his eyes, "I don't know what to do with an afflicted child."

And afflicted I was. I knew I was in trouble, and it wasn't a given that I would ever again be the person I had been before. In my desperation, I began trying to negotiate with God. *If He would help me—if He would lift me up and give me back my life—then I would surrender the rest of my life to Him. I would do whatever He wanted me to do.*

Months passed, and slowly but surely—with the help of an excellent psychiatrist, the love of family and friends, and surely God's help—my life began to come back together. I remember one day being at work and feeling once again the presence that had been around me all those months. This time, however, it didn't feel comforting so much as slightly encroaching.

Inwardly, I spoke to him: "Look, I'm really grateful to you for being here so long. You really helped me, and I'm very, very grateful. But I'm really doing well, and I'm sure you have so many other people to help. I'm absolutely fine. Thank you so, so much, and I will never forget how nice you were to me when I needed it."

I was telling God He could go now.

A few weeks later, I was at a formal cocktail party, wandering through the very large house by myself. I entered a room where a small circle of men in tuxedos were talking to one another, with drinks in their hands. One of the men turned and looked at me. Clearly, at this point, I was daydreaming. The man was Jesus.

He looked at me, and with no emotion, no recrimination, no attitude whatsoever, he said very simply, "I thought we had a deal."

And that was it. In that moment, I began my journey to a destiny that's nothing like I would ever have imagined. Whenever people ask me "How did your career begin?" I always think of Jesus at that cocktail party all those years ago.

During that period of my life, I felt like my skull was a priceless ancient vase that had been smashed. Its shattered pieces, too numerous to count, had exploded into outer space. And this turned out to be the opening to a whole new life for me. As my skull came fully back into place, it seemed that something entered my head which hadn't been there before.

Yes, that was a time when I was deeply depressed; but it also was a time when I was spiritually informed. On the other side of that dark night of my soul, I knew, saw, and understood things that I hadn't known, seen, or understood before. I've known other people who have reported similar transformations. Sometimes we have to be shaken out of our attachment to one world before we can recognize another.

WHEN SUFFERING AWAKENS US

Even the deepest darkness can reveal God's light.

Several years ago, my friend Teresa's twenty-one-year-old son was murdered. One cannot imagine a greater pain, but Teresa and her family have moved through their suffering with an eye toward life beyond it. Several years since the tragedy, Teresa is now an activist for victims' rights and a prison advocate who speaks to prisoners about emotional healing between victims and perpetrators. She told me that through this work, she has found her life's mission.

Although her anger at her son's unrepentant murderer has been a torment to her soul and remains so, the opportunity to speak to others imprisoned for the same crime has diminished her suffering. In speaking to prisoners serving life sentences for murder, Teresa has found many whose hearts are indeed repentant—and in their apologies, and their offers to be of help to her in her work, she has found solace.

One prisoner shared with her how he now fully grasps the extent of the pain he caused his victim's parents. "No matter how much time I do in prison," he told her, "I realize I cannot give them back their daughter."

The depth of his remorse made Teresa think about the depth of her own anger; she said she realized that in a very real way, this prisoner was now freer than she was—because his atonement delivered him, while her unrelenting anger has kept her bound.

She seeks to forgive because she seeks to be free, but surely none of us would doubt the difficulty of that task. God works in mysterious ways, and Teresa says that the work she does now has helped to heal her heart. Her experience working with prisoners has changed her life, opening her to the possibility that there is light in the midst of the deepest darkness. She describes her work both with prisoners and as a victims' advocate as a lifesaver, telling me, "Even given the reality of the most devastating, horrific acts of violence, I now feel that there is hope."

WHO WE CHOOSE
TO BECOME

Some powerful figures in history have been transformed in ultimately positive ways by experiences that were outwardly devastating. One of the most compelling of such stories is the life of Franklin D. Roosevelt, the 32nd president of the United States.

When he was a young man, Roosevelt was the epitome of someone who had it all. He was tall and handsome, brilliant and wealthy, married with several children. His cousin Theodore had been president of the United States, and his own career seemed guaranteed to go as far as he chose to take it.

One day in 1921, while on vacation at his family lake house in Canada, Roosevelt took a swim. Within hours of returning home he was suffering chills, within days his limbs were numb, and within weeks he was diagnosed with polio.

Yet this tragedy was not the end of his story; in a profound way, it was just the beginning. Roosevelt would never walk again without the help of iron braces and canes, but from the crucible of his suffering he emerged as someone who did as much to ameliorate the suffering of others as has anyone in history.

Three years after his diagnosis, Roosevelt traveled to a resort in Warm Springs, Georgia, known for its eighty-eight-degree natural springs. Its hot waters eased his physical pain, but at least as importantly, the kindness of those he met there lifted his spirits. Few others at Warm Springs had ever heard of the Roosevelts of Hyde Park, New York. They didn't know of FDR's wealth or care about his power. To those he met at Warm Springs, many of them poor, he was just another sufferer, a saddened man who needed the waters to soothe his pain. They cared for him simply because he was a human being who shared their affliction. Through that experience, Roosevelt came to know, and to depend upon, the kindness of people he most probably would never have met otherwise.

This is a common theme—a recurrent archetype—on the journey out of suffering. People arrive to help us in our darkest hours, and they often come oddly disguised. Someone we might never have met, or respected—much less looked to for help—ends up giving us pivotal assistance that we could not have gotten elsewhere. People at a ramshackle resort helped heal Roosevelt in ways that all the doctors at the best medical institutions could not do. Not all God's angels have letters on their doors announcing that they are angels. Nothing humbles us like being helped by people whose help we never thought we would need.

Years later, when Roosevelt became president, he was faced with the suffering of millions left poverty-stricken by the crash of the stock market in 1929. Given his own socioeconomic background, he may not have had a deep, visceral compassion for the millions of unemployed people struggling during the Great Depression. He was a very rich man from a very rich family, and he could easily have walled himself off emotionally from those who suffered the most at that time. They were not the likes of the Roosevelts of Hyde Park; but they were very much the likes of the people Roosevelt had known, and come to depend upon, in Warm Springs, Georgia.

Now it was his turn to give back. His empathy for the hardships endured by average Americans at that time inspired the New Deal, an array of social and economic programs that brought relief to millions of people. Roosevelt was not a perfect man—there were many left outside the circle of his compassion—but someone with less empathy would not have accomplished the New Deal, nor perhaps even tried. My own father grew up in poverty and spoke admiringly of Roosevelt throughout his life as the man who had saved my father's family from ruin. Until the day he died in 1995, anytime you asked Daddy who he voted for on Election Day, his response was always the same: "I voted for Roosevelt."

Roosevelt's suffering helped turn him into the man he needed to be to alleviate the suffering of millions. When tragedies occur, we don't always get an answer to the question, "Why did this happen to me?" But we can always question what blessing can still come from the experience.

We cannot always choose whether or not we suffer, but we can choose whether or not our suffering will have been in vain. From the person who loses his or her eyesight and then becomes an advocate for the blind; to the parent who forms a foundation in his or her late child's memory; to the athlete who loses limbs and then founds an athletic organization for others similarly challenged—a key to transcending our suffering is to use it as a blessing on the lives of others.

It would be a mistake to idealize suffering, but it would also be a mistake to diminish its relevance to the formation of character. In the words of poet Khalil Gibran, "Out of suffering have emerged the strongest souls; the most massive characters are seared with scars."

Too many people are sad about unimportant things, perhaps *because* they won't let themselves be sad about the larger tragedies of life. Carl Jung said, "Neurosis is always a substitute for legitimate suffering." In allowing our hearts to be pierced by instances of genuine suffering, both in our own lives and in the lives of others, we counterintuitively become more available to some of life's most exquisite opportunities for happiness.

Nothing makes us stronger than having climbed out of the deepest valleys of despair to the highest peaks of joy, and nothing pushes us from behind like angels reminding us not to forget the others who are scaling the mountain with us. Once having reached the peak, we find that we're no longer crying—and even more importantly, we find we're no longer alone.

Once we embrace the realization that happiness 24/7 is not promised in life, we gain a more mature acceptance of life's ups and downs. Things do not always go as we wish, not everything is under our control, and no matter what happens, life on earth is a temporary ride. When we are honest with ourselves, we recognize that every day holds the potential for heartbreak. But joy doesn't rest on trusting that every day will unfold as we wish; sometimes it rests on simply appreciating the fact that today, on this day, everything is fine. The rough times in our lives can lead us to feeling, among other things, greater gratitude for life when it goes well. Having lost things that were precious, we learn to be much happier with the things that remain. Suffering can leave us scarred, yet still, in almost mysterious ways, we can become better people for having gone through it. Sometimes the fact that "I'll never be the same again" is not such a bad thing. We won't be who we used to be, but who we become now is completely up to us.

Dear God,

Please make of my life

A beautiful thing.

Guide me on an illumined journey

From the darkness of the world

To the light that is You.

Make of me a conduit

Of good

That I might help transform the world.

Set my feet upon a hero's journey

And my heart on an enlightened path.

Amen

SPIRITUAL MATURITY

When suffering has led us to the realization that to find ultimate answers we should go to God, the question then becomes, but where do I go to find God?

Now, in the twenty-first century, our great religious stories bear a new and modern look. For they are more practically applicable to the issues of contemporary life than many people realize. They can be freed from the lifeless containers of institutionalized religion or mere academic pursuit to which they're often relegated. We can breathe the life of immediate, practical relevance into what otherwise can be perceived as mere metaphor or concept.

One doesn't have to be clergy, a monk, a teacher, or anything special to search for enlightenment. The call of the soul is universal. It doesn't require particular beliefs because it is an experience, an understanding that begins as an abstraction and then leads to what *A Course in Miracles* calls a " journey without distance" from the head to the heart.

Often, people want to know the how-tos of enlightenment, as though a few easy steps should be able to do it. But forgiveness, compassion, atonement, and faith are not always easy steps—even when we understand their importance. Enlightenment involves more than a collection of metaphysical data; it involves the actual practice, application, and embodiment of love.

The purpose of religion is not just to tell stories, but to change our lives. And the religious experience is just that: an *experience.* Only when that experience is an opening to love does it truly have anything to do with God. And God's truth cannot be monopolized by any group or institution, no matter what those groups say and no matter how many centuries they've been saying it.

The purpose of religion is to bind us back to our right minds, which is the mystical intelligence of the universe. *A Course in Miracles* says that, in their essence, religion and psychotherapy are the same thing. Regardless of what words we use, salvation lies in the healing of our minds.

Enlightenment, then, applies to earth as much as to heaven. *A Course in Miracles* says that the line in the Bible "Heaven and earth shall pass away" means that in time they will no longer exist as two separate states. The realms of practical experience and ideal consciousness will be as one.

Enlightenment isn't a learning, but an *un*learning. It's a process, usually involving a lot of trial and error, through which we come to reject the ego's guidance and accept love's guidance instead. It's not just an expansion of who we are, but the dissolution of a false self that's been masquerading as who we are. As an egoless state of consciousness, it is actually our natural state of being. And while few of us can say that we've attained it on a consistent basis, most of us have had moments when we've been there—moments when we felt free to love and to be loved. Until we become enlightened masters, we will still make mistakes and stumble and fall with everyone else. But we can become people for whom the good days, the happy times, are more the rule than the exception. And that itself is a miracle.

Light, according to *A Course in Miracles*, means "understanding." The enlightened mind is the mind that understands. It understands that only love is real, and nothing else exists. It understands that illusions dissolve in the presence of love. It understands that we, and everything about our lives, can change.

Enlightenment and miracles naturally go together, because the mind that's healed of fear is a vessel of love, and the mind that is a vessel of love works miracles. When light begins to dawn on our minds, the darkness of the deepest night recedes.

EMBRACING MIRACLES

When we forgive, when we atone, when we apologize, when we own our mistakes, when we extend compassion, we are not just being "nice." We're following immutable laws of the universe. Spiritual principles are based on internal laws of consciousness as fixed and unalterable as any laws of science. We know that holding a grievance toward another will block a miracle as surely as letting go of a book from our hands will make it fall onto the ground.

This is particularly important when we're depressed, because at no time are we more tempted to thoughts of hopelessness and negativity. Thoughts like "Nothing will ever be good again" and "All hope is lost"—not to mention, "I hate those people for how they treated me"—are mental meanderings that disrupt the flow of miracles.

Week after week, for more than thirty years, I've spoken to audiences about how love works miracles. As often as not, someone in the audience is crying, trying to lift themselves up from the regions of despair—heartbreak over a broken love affair, the pain of a bitter divorce, the diagnosis of a life-threatening illness, financial ruin, the acceptance of a loved one's, or their own, addiction, and so forth. My message to them is never that they shouldn't cry. Having been where they are, that's the last thing I would say to them. But I would say, as others have said to me during the times of my own suffering, that God works miracles. And that He never runs out of them.

Some periods of life are not easy. They call for deep inner work and emotional heavy lifting. This might mean you have to accept what feels unacceptable, or forgive what feels like the unforgivable. It might mean taking a painful look at yourself, or being open to change in areas where you can't imagine yourself changing. Spiritual comfort doesn't derive from simply throwing a little white light around an issue. It's not like you grasp a spiritual principle or two and voilà, your pain is gone. Rather, you start learning and applying the principles and voilà, you're on your way.

Spiritual work is *not* an easy way to cope, like something we grab on to as a substitute for *serious* psychological remedy. It is a walk through what can be a very deep, dark psychic jungle, knowing that monsters lurk among the trees but with the hero's dedication to conquering them. Spirituality isn't the purview of the weak; it's the purview of the brave.

The spiritual journey dredges up the mud of our subconscious fears, yet it does so in order to remove them. In the words of Carl Jung, "One does not become enlightened by imagining figures of light, but by making the darkness conscious." Fear and negativity that remain hidden in the darkness of our unconsciousness have the power to hurt us; when brought to the light of conscious awareness, they can then be surrendered to God and miraculously transformed.

While all this is going on, it's understandable that we're depressed. But that doesn't necessarily mean something is *wrong*. It simply means that the work is being done: something is being looked at, something is being endured, and ultimately something is being healed. Sadness during the process is natural; we're looking at things that are not easy to look at, and changing in ways that involve vulnerability before God and sometimes before other people as well.

Sometimes we have to walk a painful path in order to get to the path's end, but the experience becomes a holy crucible when we make the walk with God.

MYSTICAL TRADITION AND SPIRITUAL TRUTH

Mysticism is the path of the heart. It is not a religion, but rather a holy river of universal themes that runs through the great religious and spiritual systems of the world. It does not posit an external broker for our spiritual lives in the form of a human being or institution, but rather the presence of a divinely inspired guidance system that dwells within us all.

Spiritual conversion is not to a doctrine or dogma, but to a different way of seeing. We gain new eyes when we extend our perception beyond the darkness of the world to the light that lies beyond. Spiritual light is the transcendent field of infinite possibilities that exist beyond circumstances that the ego would claim are all sewn up. That is how spiritual truth lights our way out of darkness. It restores our hope by realigning our thoughts with the idea that in God all things are possible.

Regardless of the terrible perversions of religious truth that the ego so slyly promulgates, the great religious stories remain keys that unlock our psychological mysteries. Religious stories are not just symbols; they are mystical codes. When understood metaphysically, they remove the veil that hides the light kept hidden by the ego. The great religious figures of history reveal common undeniable truths.

Whether universal principles are articulated in Christianity or Alcoholics Anonymous, Judaism or *A Course in Miracles*, Islam or Buddhism or Hinduism or wherever, they are ours to mine for spiritual treasure if we wish. A contemporary generation of seekers now looks to those universal truths for help in guiding us out of the dark morass that is this time in human history.

The great religious traditions are spiritual renditions of the hero's journey. This journey is our common search for meaning within a world often dominated by the meaningless. The goal of a spiritual life is the attainment of inner peace, achieved through the application of loving principles to our everyday concerns. These principles are invisible forces that, when applied, wield unlimited power to change our lives.

Great religious stories reveal eternally relevant information. They guide us through the confusion of mortal existence to the clarity of spiritual truth. There is one spiritual Truth with a capital *T*, spoken in many different ways and told through many different filters, both secular and religious. Like a classic Cole Porter song sung by Frank Sinatra in 1943 and then again by U2 in 2010, every age has the right—and a responsibility to itself—to refresh its

understanding of spiritual principles according to its own perspective and experience. It is said in the Jewish tradition that every
generation must rediscover God for itself.

One thing that does not change, generation to generation, is that
people suffer and look for suffering's end. Suffering is at the core
of all the great religious tales because it is at the core of the human
experience. The lives of Buddha, Moses, and Jesus are three that
created explosions of light within the collective psyche of humanity, all bearing witness to, enduring, and transforming the pain of
living. From Buddha's observation of suffering when he first left his
father's house, to Moses guiding the Israelites out of their suffering
in Egypt, to the suffering of Jesus on the cross—all three point to
the suffering of the world, and to our deliverance from it.

Exploring Buddha, Moses, and Jesus through the lens of miracle-
minded thinking adds a dimension of understanding to the truths
they reveal. Their stories, their suffering, and the deliverance they
provided, illumine our experience and expand our hearts.

Suffering the trials and tribulations of the world, or identifying
with those who suffer them, spiritually transforms us. Through their
own suffering, great spiritual figures have been transformed and then
gifted the ages with divine illumination. It was not simply that Buddha,
or Moses, or Jesus became privy to some abstract understanding that
they could pass along to the rest of us. Something much deeper than
that occurred, of course. They were themselves in-formed. They received divine truths not abstractly but viscerally, not just through
intellect but through experience, in order to become conduits for the
transmission of that information into the minds of others.

Because all minds are joined and mind itself is eternal, when anyone, anywhere at any time, attains a state of consciousness in which the spiritual world penetrates the material, the opportunity is created for anyone else, anywhere and at any time, to do the same. The consciousness of a great religious figure is a tunnel of perpetual energy—a door, a vortex, or whatever words we use to describe it—through which others can more easily enter into the same higher consciousness. Like evolutionary elders, they achieve a state toward which all of us are moving; their having done so makes our journeys more achievable. Their story, their mission, becomes an imprint on our own psyches that carries transformational power to transfigure us as it transfigured them.

We're not asked to reenact the suffering of the great religious figures, but merely to learn from it so that we too might come to embody the messages they received.

When we ourselves are suffering—at the mercy of spiritual ignorance, slaves to our own egos, enduring physical disease or injury, or any other deep trial—spiritual light is the hand of God reaching down to lift us up. Great spiritual teachings are lights that cast out darkness from our minds, ladders of consciousness out of the depths of our despair. The religious experience—not a mere adherence to doctrine or dogma, but rather a genuine encounter with God when we call out to Him in our helplessness and pain—is the opening of a door through which we exit the realm of spiritual darkness.

This is not to glorify suffering, but simply to recognize that even there, God *is*. Often, the things that mark the end of one life are simply the beginnings of a new one. Unless we allow our suffering to teach us what it *can* teach us, however—total and utter reliance on God's Love as the one and only source of our happiness, not in some things but in all things—then our pain will never seem to have been anything more than a result of random chaos with no ultimate meaning. Like everything else, it will have whatever meaning we ascribe to it. To love, above all else, is the meaning of our lives—to place the extension of compassion for other sentient beings at the top of our list when we consider why we were born, why we wake up every morning, why we do what we do, and why we go where we go. Anything else is ultimately meaningless and will never be powerful enough to end our suffering or provide a way to true peace. We might not ever attain, at least in this lifetime, the enlightened consciousness of Buddha, or Moses, or Jesus; but the effort itself makes life worth living, brings suffering to an end, and makes happiness a fundamental and achievable goal.

NINE

The Light
of Buddha

*B*uddha simply claimed that he taught about suffering, its origin, and its cessation. "That's all I teach," he said. He taught that all life is suffering, and the only antidote to that suffering is infinite compassion, or enlightenment. The only way out of our suffering is to identify with the suffering of others; the only meaning to our suffering is that it might expand our hearts so we can.

Buddha was born Prince Siddhartha, the son of a king told by a renowned seer upon the birth of his son that the child would grow up to be either a great conquering king or a great holy man. The king was adamant that Siddhartha should grow up to follow in his royal foot-steps, so he sought to keep his son shielded from religious teachings throughout his life. He enclosed his palace compound within thick walls, allowing only pleasurable things to exist there in the hopes that a luxurious lifestyle would keep suffering from Siddhartha's sight. From educational opportunities to sensual pleasures, over the years Siddhartha was exposed to everything his father believed would make him happy and keep him tied to the royal household. He reached the age of twenty-nine with little or no exposure to life outside this opulent environment.

Despite the abundance of worldly pleasures he experienced throughout his life, a restlessness began to grow inside Siddhartha's heart. He felt something was missing in his life though he had no idea what it was. He knew there was more to human existence than the material grandeur he had been raised with . . . something he hadn't seen but that he needed to see. One day he set out on a series of rides throughout the countryside, seeking to discover the world that lay beyond the walls of his father's house.

On his rides, he saw an aged man, a sick man, and a corpse. For the first time in his life, Siddhartha saw the realities of aging, disease, and death. He was profoundly changed. Returning to the palace, he saw things there in a different light. He realized that even the musicians and dancers, all the objects of luxury we use to keep suffering at bay, in time deteriorate and turn back into dust. It is a mere illusion to think otherwise. Even the son who had been born in his absence brought him no joy; in fact, his very name, Rahula, means "fetter." Siddhartha was now seeking something beyond what his former life could give him.

During his rides Siddhartha had seen a wandering ascetic— someone who had renounced the world and sought release from the fear of death and suffering—and he chose this as his path. He stole away from the palace, shaved his head, and put on a beggar's robe. Thus he began his search for enlightenment.

Siddhartha's path, like all of our paths, was not easy. The divestment of his illusions took him through various forms of suffering, as he was forced to face down the demons of the delusional self. The false gods of the ego mind—embodied in Buddhism as the demon Mara, which means "destruction"—sought to fool, betray, and ensnare him. As they do us all.

Yet Siddhartha cleaved to his recognition of the eternal that lies beyond the temporary, the clarity beyond passion, and the truth beyond illusion. The great mental battle between the forces of truth and falsehood that raged within him is revered as his approach to enlightenment beneath the Bodhi tree. Though Mara mentally tortured him, the earth itself promised to bear him witness, and Mara was ultimately defeated. Siddhartha's eyes were opened to the true nature of reality, and he became the Buddha, or Awakened One.

Buddha saw, experienced, and transcended suffering. He saw attachment to the world as the source of our suffering and infinite compassion as the key to transcending it. The teachings that emerged from this realization are a path by which billions of souls have pierced the veil of illusion that blinds us to ultimate reality, for in remembering his journey we are awakened to our own. Buddha's enlightenment is a door through which we can transcend our own suffering as he transcended his. The world is an immeasurably more beautiful place for all the light he brought into the world.

THE FOUR NOBLE TRUTHS AND
THE EIGHTFOLD PATH

The spiritual journey is a gentle reinterpretation of the world, the replacement of an increasingly outdated internal operating system with the far more sophisticated patterns of enlightened thinking. All suffering emanates from the activity of the mind when it is attached to the illusions of the world; only infinite compassion releases us from these attachments and delivers us to inner peace.

Buddhism, like *A Course in Miracles,* teaches that the three-dimensional world is a vast illusion. The mortal world is but a veil in front of a truer truth; the veil is lifted not when we look away from it, but when we look through it with different eyes.

The Buddhist Four Noble Truths and the Eightfold Path are guides to our deliverance from suffering, as we embrace the ways of enlightenment, or right-mindedness. "Embracing the ways of enlightenment" and "praying for a miracle" are fundamentally the same thing.

I have vivid memories of two particular instances when, feeling very down, I prayed for a miracle. Both times, literally within minutes of my saying the prayer, something happened that changed my mood. Both times I was asked, while in the midst of my pain, to do something for someone else. At first I thought, "Oh God, I can't do this," then realized that the request was in fact the answer to *my* prayer! The opportunity to do something for someone else was an opportunity to *get over myself.* And it worked. Any thought that posits our own perceived needs as more important than those of others is a thought of separation, and will not lead to happiness. A serious spiritual path is a practice of consistent emotional deliverance to the love that replaces fear, not merely in response to specific situations but as an attitude toward life. Such practice makes suffering, when it does appear, both endurable and transformable. Only by detaching from the illusions of the world—what Buddha called *maya*—can we transcend the thoughts and feelings that too often sour our experience of being human.

Buddha's Four Noble Truths were the realizations that (1) things of this world can provide only temporary happiness at best; (2) suffering is caused by our attachment to the things of this world; (3) we can be liberated from our attachments to the things of this world and thus freed from our suffering; and (4) through the Eightfold Path, or the Middle Way—choosing neither extreme luxury nor extreme self-denial—we can be free of suffering. The Eightfold Path includes *Right Understanding, Right Intention, Right Speech, Right Action, Right Livelihood, Right Effort, Right Mindfulness,* and *Right Concentration.* These are not just theoretical; they are keys to a peaceful mind.

Right Understanding

Buddhism proclaims that only ultimate reality is real, and it is our attachment to that which is unreal that causes us to suffer. Life simply is what it is. It is not events that cause us to suffer, so much as how we *perceive* those events.

Someone might have been unkind to us, and because of this we suffer—or so we think. But if only love is real, then the unkindness does not exist except in the realm of illusion. *Right Understanding* means we see that since the worldly personality is part of the illusion, we do not have to limit our perceptions to the personality that caused us pain. Through *Right Understanding* we can extend our perceptions beyond what the physical senses perceive to the truer reality that lies beyond.

For example, I can choose to close my heart in response to being hurt by you but my pain is then a result not of your having closed your heart to me, but of my having closed my heart to you. I cannot be hurt by something the existence of which I am not attached to. I cannot be affected by something to which I refuse to accord reality.

The words *disciple* and *discipline* come from the same root; it takes discipline to focus on what is fundamentally true despite appearances. *Right Understanding* means refusing to defer to a reality that does not actually exist, despite the fact that our physical senses insist that it does.

The body's eyes insist that an airplane gets smaller the farther away it flies from us, yet obviously it doesn't. Our physical senses are indicators of a three-dimensional reality that is a mortal hallucination. The spiritual journey is a shift from the outer eye to an inner eye, as we extend our perceptions beyond the veil of illusion to a truer truth that lies beyond.

Releasing the universe from our grasping mind allows us to see it as it truly is. In Buddhism, that state of mental and emotional release is called nirvana. It is an enlightened state of awareness in which the celestial order is restored, karma is undone, and inner peace is possible.

Once when a magazine published a story about me containing embarrassing lies and fabrications, I was devastated. The night it came out, I saw a famous pop star at a dinner and these were his first words to me: "Marianne, pretend you were in Japan. You didn't even read it." He said those words so declaratively, with such force, that in that moment I truly realized I had a choice. Since then I have thought of his advice often. To this day, I will sometimes say to myself, "Marianne, pretend you were in Japan," when I am tempted to misunderstand a situation and allow it to defeat me.

Right Intention

The power of intention has become widely recognized, but it's a power that can be used for the purposes of both spirit and ego. Used by spirit, intention is a tool in co-creating a more loving world. Used by ego, it is a tool for simply trying to get whatever it is we think we want. Using the power of the mind to make something happen out of sheer self-will, is not necessarily spiritual. That which does not serve love does not serve the spiritual unfolding of the universe, for the spiritual unfolding of the universe is love and love only.

The intentions of the ego mind are that we get this or that, or make this or that happen. *Right Intention* is a higher vibration entirely. It is the intention that only love prevail for all living things.

The Buddha spoke of both *Right Intention* and *Wrong Intention. Right Intention* means the intention to be an instrument of healing; wrong intention means to be an instrument of harm. Neutrality is not an option. All thought creates an effect on some level. What we don't intend for loving purposes will be appropriated for fearful ones.

We might tell ourselves we had the best of intentions in a situation simply because we didn't consciously intend to hurt someone.

Often, when someone hurts us these days they say, "I didn't intend to hurt you," as though that's an *apology*. But according to the Buddha, it's not enough to *not intend* ill will; we must *intend* goodwill.

Once we even slightly recognize to what degree every thought we think affects the vibratory field around us, we realize that even what the world doesn't see or hear, the universe still registers. There is a documentary called *The True Cost* that reveals the horrible injustices perpetrated against people in sweatshops supplying the "fast fashion" industry. The film perfectly illustrates the conundrum of intentionality. When I buy a twelve-dollar pair of jeans at a trendy discount store, I certainly don't intend to hurt anyone; I simply intend to find a cool pair of jeans at a good price. After I saw that film, I embraced a higher intention; in this instance, *Right Intention* means no longer shopping at huge chain stores that sell cheap items at the expense of people working in sweatshops who are treated like little more than slaves on the other side of the world.

From how factory workers are treated and paid in many countries, to the cruel treatment of animals, to even driving alone when we could just as easily carpool, Buddha's precept of *Right Intention* calls us to a higher level of consciousness that most of us have yet to reach. Certainly I haven't. Yet we can try to improve at whatever rate we can. Simply living in modern society poses constant challenges to the concept of *Right Intention*. The harm we do to others and the harm we *allow* to be done to others are added to the karmic burden we collectively carry forward.

Right Intention is important to understanding how to heal our suffering because it encourages us to rethink the causes of our pain as well as an appropriate response to it. When we understand how to distinguish between right and wrong intention, we alter the way we deal with our own suffering and how we view suffering throughout the world. We can *intend* to be instruments of good, even when we least feel like doing so.

"You mean now, while I'm dealing with my own pain, I have to think about how I'm affecting others?" If you want to heal, the answer is yes.

Right Speech

Right Speech is an important aspect of right-mindedness. The words we say emanate subtle and not-so-subtle influence on us and on those around us. The right use of words is an important tool on the path to transforming our suffering.

Buddha identified four keys to *Right Speech:* words spoken with affection, with honesty, for the good of others, and with the intent of doing good.

Right Speech applies even to how we speak about ourselves. All of us need to talk through things, of course. But while processing is important, sometimes we can inadvertently cross the line from harmlessness to harm, saying self-denigrating things like, "I was so stupid! I'm such a failure!" But an attack on ourselves is no less blasphemous than an attack on others. Although it's necessary to process life's disappointments, such processing is best done in the sacred space of professional counseling, anonymous support groups, or the most trusted friendships. It's important that we seek to be kind to ourselves and others, even as we seek to be honest. With every word we say we're forming thoughts, and every thought creates form on some level.

Of course we all have negative thoughts, but the point is to own them, to bear witness to them, and then to surrender them. The ego's plan for getting out of pain is to project its source onto others, but this thwarts our healing. It's not a question of whether or not we have the "right" to negative feelings; of course we do. The issue is how we choose to manage our personal power. Words have power both to heal and to harm.

It's inaccurate to think that it doesn't matter what I say because "I don't really mean it" or "He'll never know that I said that." Think of the universe as having ears. Every word we say bears the imprint of its power, regardless who is listening. I remember when we were children and would say to each other, "Take that back!" whenever someone said something we didn't like. We clearly knew instinctively that words are powerful. Even today, how often do we say "Cancel, cancel!" when we hear a friend make a negative comment? And for good reason.

Right Speech is more than what we say; it's also *how* we say it. I've been criticized for speaking in a way that hurt other people's feelings, when at the time the farthest thing from my mind was the intention to hurt anyone. I had thought I was merely stating facts. But the line between a "share" and an "attack" needs to be monitored closely; what we might feel is simply blunt when we say it might feel harsh to the person who hears it. If our words carry the energy of an attack, then it doesn't matter whether what we're saying is *true*. If we're attacking someone, then we're wrong even if we're right. How true the saying that honesty without compassion is brutality.

The word *communication* contains the word "commune," and if we're not communing, then we're really not communicating at all. Feeling attacked, the person to whom we're speaking will not feel we simply "shared our truth." Understandably, they will defensively shut their hearts to us as they feel we shut our hearts to them, and that, of course, will shut their ears. We will not be heard; we will merely be resented. And the cycle of violence will go on.

Learning to be as honest and authentic as possible, yet taking responsibility for the heart space between ourselves and someone else, is essential to enlightenment.

Right Speech also includes recognizing the power of not speaking at all. In the words of Mahatma Gandhi, "Speak only if it improves upon the silence." One of the fruits of meditation is enabling a still and quiet mind, no small thing in a world where far too many people seem to lack impulse control. The ego wants to say it, and wants to say it *now.* Send that text! Send that email! Make that phone call! Tell 'em what you think! But simply having a thought, no matter how true it might be, does not necessarily mean it should be shared or shared right now.

If, when hurt, we surrender our feelings to God, then we may or may not feel moved to speak at all. When and if there are things to be said, things that would reflect the highest good, then we'll be guided not only on what to say, but also on when and how to say it. That makes all the difference in the world.

Negative gossip is another issue that applies to *Right Speech;* basically, if a person we're talking about wouldn't be glad to hear what we're saying about them, then we probably shouldn't be saying it. I remember my mother used to quote Thumper in *Bambi,* "If you don't have something nice to say, then don't say anything at all." Because all minds are joined, subconsciously everyone knows everything. Whatever we're saying about anyone, on some level they know it. Every word spoken—about ourselves, about others, about anything at all—carries the force of the thought behind it. You know that old saying: "Stick and stones can break my bones, but words can never hurt me"? Well it isn't true. Verbal violence is still violence, and words can hurt a lot.

Right Action

Right Action is the directive to act only in ways that are in harmony with the universe. It stems automatically from the ultimate reality of who we are, which is infinite compassion.

Too often in today's world, we think of what to do only in terms of whether or not it will get us what we want. But *Right Action* is a call to a higher motivation for our behavior. Some things we should do for no other reason than that they're the right thing to do—not because we'll get something out of it, and not because other people will know about it and applaud. We should do it for no other reason than that it's in alignment with integrity, honesty, goodness, and love.

This means, obviously, that we do not kill, steal, or have sex with people who are bound emotionally or ethically to others. We seek to be honest, to act impeccably, to respect our agreements. Every cause has an effect. Anything we do will be done to us, and what we withhold from others will be withheld from us. There is no greater call to *Right Action* than the Golden Rule: Do unto others as you would have them do unto you. Because they, or someone else, *will.*

Particularly when we're in pain, or when we feel the need to make something happen, the temptation is great to compromise with the principle of *Right Action.* Yet once we truly understand that every action calls forth a reaction—whether that action is ever seen or known by anyone else—then we understand that there's no compromise with righteousness that does not ultimately compromise our own good.

Sometimes we might be asked to do something and find ourselves thinking: "Oh God, I don't have the time! I don't have the energy! I don't have the bandwidth!" It's also very common these days to run into people who ask us to consider whether we might be "giving too much." But our response should always be determined by what we truly feel in our hearts. And the universe will support us. When your heart expands, your life expands; and when your heart constricts, your life constricts.

The ego, or Mara, often argues that our good lies in avoiding our responsibilities, cutting corners, resisting the ethical path. But only the good promulgates the good, and proactively seeking to do right by others is the only way we can experience the universe doing right by us. When we're depressed is *not* the time to lessen our spiritual vigilance. By practicing spiritual principles, particularly during times of great sorrow, we conspire with the universe in putting our lives back on track.

Sometimes *Right Action* means we have to apologize to someone who is the last person in the world we want to apologize to. Or go somewhere that is the last place in the world we want to go. But if we feel in our hearts that it's "the right thing to do," then we will be blessed by having done it. A dysfunction very prevalent in our society is the notion that we should do something only if it *feels* good, or if we think it will get us something of value. Such a notion springs from spiritual ignorance and is the farthest thing from the truth.

Giving ourselves emotional permission to just do whatever we want is not freedom, but license. It does not liberate, but imprisons. *Right Action*—trying to do the right thing—is the only path of enlightenment, because it flows from the guidance of the heart.

Right Livelihood

Right Livelihood is the principle of making ethical career choices; it means not making a living in ways that harm people or animals, because doing so would obstruct enlightenment. Once we see our work as a channel for the extension of our love into the world, we seek to make a living in a way that aligns with a higher calling.

Challenges to the principle of *Right Livelihood* confront many of us at work these days. We might wonder whether we should speak up about an unethical practice on the part of the company we work for but we're afraid we might lose our job if we do, and we think "it's not that big a deal anyway." Or we might overcharge for a product because we really need that extra money this month. Or indirectly promote violence by working on a gratuitously violent commercial, television show, or movie. Or sell an item that we know in our hearts will not deliver on what it promises.

Given critical ethical lapses in today's global economy—huge corporate conglomerates putting their own short-term economic gain before the health and well-being of the world's majority of inhabitants and of the planet itself—the issue of *Right Livelihood* has collective significance too. If we as individuals do all we can to be ethical in the way we conduct our own professional affairs, is that enough? Or are we not called to consider the larger picture of an economic system that is increasingly predicated on increased profits for the few at the expense of the many?

It's easy to slide on this one, to think that if we don't hurt anyone directly through what we do for a living, then surely we reap no negative consequences. But if we indirectly support an unethical business by providing a professional support service, for instance, then indeed we're violating the principle of *Right Livelihood*. No principle on Buddha's Eightfold Path is more relevant to the future of humanity than that which encourages the advanced nations of the world to consider the negative karma that accrues when we place business at the service of greed as opposed to love.

Much unnecessary suffering in the world today—from individuals cast aside by the global economy to economic crises brought about by unethical banking practices—has been caused by a lack of *Right Livelihood*, not necessarily on our part, but on the part of systems of which we're a part. Spiritually, we cannot afford to care only for ourselves in relation to money or anything else. I saw a protester involved with the Occupy movement holding a sign that said, *"Wall Street Should Practice Right Livelihood."* Indeed.

Simply knowing that *Right Livelihood* is part of the Eightfold Path puts the issue in front of us in a significant way. That is the gift of Buddhism, as of any spiritual teaching. It doesn't put our spirituality "over there," in some corner far away from our day-to-day existence.

If we all try just a little bit harder to apply this principle more consistently, then changes both large and small will begin to occur in our financial affairs. The violation of this principle is at the heart of a lot of negative karma in our lives, as individuals and as a society. Beginning to honor the importance of *Right Livelihood* would have a radically positive effect on us all.

Right Effort

Right Effort is the proactive cultivation of enlightenment as the only antidote to the neurotic obsessions of the ego mind. The reason we want to practice it is because the mind is extremely powerful in whatever direction it's turned. A mind that is not conscious and proactively attuned to the effort of right-mindedness is put at the service of wrong-mindedness. Mara is always seeking to triumph over love and uses any opportunity to take advantage of our lack of vigilance.

When we're depressed, Mara specializes in negative thoughts and feelings such as victimization, hopelessness, cynicism, anger, revenge, attack, and blame. It takes effort to transcend such thoughts, to recognize them for the ego forces that they are, and to work at thinking otherwise. During a time of sadness, a commitment to *Right Effort* is more important than ever because one of the things that's particularly debilitating about sadness is that it drains us of our energy. Mara feeds on laziness, procrastination, rationalization, and self-indulgence.

Sometimes *Right Effort* is to apologize to someone; sometimes it's to start a payment plan to pay off a bill; sometimes it's to clear the air in a relationship; sometimes it's to start exercising more, or meditating more, or reading more; sometimes it's to do service; sometimes it's to write a thank-you note; sometimes it's to do something gracious that you simply haven't thought you had time to do; sometimes it's to participate in your responsibilities as a citizen; sometimes it's to donate to a good cause; sometimes it's to clean up your house; sometimes it's to call a friend or family member. In our hearts, we usually know what to do. *Right Effort* simply means that we choose to do it.

Sometimes, when suffering has us hunched over in pain, the *Right Effort* called for is merely to get up each morning and put one foot in front of the other, to muster enough faith in possibility to simply make it through another day. And that itself is a good thing. Whatever *Right Effort* we can make on behalf of compassion for ourselves and others, the universe will receive it and will respond in kind. When we make the effort to follow principles of enlightenment, the powers of enlightenment empower us.

Right Mindfulness

Mindfulness is an idea that's in vogue today, its popularization having produced treatises on everything from mindful parenting to mindful work to mindful divorce. Being mindful is certainly the apex of the spiritual journey, as it's the mental alignment from whence all compassion comes.

Right Mindfulness means "right awareness" or "right attention." It means disciplining the mind to remember what is eternal beyond the temporary, embracing ultimate reality beyond the illusions of

the world. *Right Mindfulness* is the attainment of a state of consciousness beyond all concepts, symbols, illusions, and false associations
of the mortal mind. It is the intersection of the human and divine,
the perfect alignment of the mortal mind with the Mind of God.
There, in that place, there is no impulse to wrong-minded thought
or behavior, no vulnerability to Mara's dance of death, no hysterical voices screaming in our heads. The mindful mind is the whole,
or holy, mind.

Not too long ago, I was visiting New Delhi. I was supposed to
meet someone for lunch in the lobby of a hotel, but I didn't know
what he looked like since we had only communicated via email. The
lobby was quite busy and I was late for the appointment. Looking
around, I began to feel quite anxious. A lovely young woman who
worked for the hotel came up and asked if she could help. I told her
I was quite stressed due to the circumstances, and didn't know what I
should do. She told me I should go into a corner of the lobby, sit
down, and find my calm; then surely it would become clear to me
what I should do next. I chuckled and thought to myself, "Right.
I'm supposed to know that."

It can take years of meditation and practice to attain *Right
Mindfulness* on a consistent basis. Sometimes we are simply delivered to such a state, like a gift of grace at certain moments when
we least expect it. Whether we are looking ahead to the goal of
Right Mindfulness, or remembering the moments when we knew we
were there, it shines like a beacon of divine possibility for all of us.
Buddha attained it, and in following his path, we are following that
beacon to our enlightenment too.

Right Concentration

Right Concentration is the correct focus of the mind. By focusing the mind on what is true, we not only rise above suffering, but we transform it. It involves the cultivation of a quiet mind to still the forces of chaos within us.

Buddhist meditation, like *A Course in Miracles* and all serious spiritual practices, is a tool by which a suffering mind transcends its agony. Such practices train us to stay focused on the present when the mind is obsessed with past and future; to stay focused on compassion when the ego is obsessed with another person's guilt; to stay focused on the deeper realities of life beyond the illusions of the world.

A Course in Miracles says that we achieve so little because our minds are undisciplined. We're far too tolerant of the ego when it wanders into the temptation of negative, critical thought. Buddhists use meditation to focus the mind on what is really true as a way of dissolving that which is not.

There's a Buddhist tale of a warlord who sent his minions into a monastery to announce that he was taking it over as his personal possession, and that all the monks there were to leave. One monk, however, refused to go. When his minions reported his refusal to the warlord, he asked, "Did you tell him he would be killed if he didn't do as I say?" The minions said they had indeed relayed that message, but the monk didn't budge from his seated position.

The warlord then decided to enter the monastery and speak to the monk himself.

He brandished his sword and pressed it lightly at the monk's throat. "Did you know," he barked, "that I could take this sword and cut you open from top to bottom?"

The monk looked at the warlord and answered very calmly, "Did you know that I could let you?"

With that, the warlord dropped his sword and fell to his knees. Realizing he was in the presence of a spiritual master, he gave up his life of violence and began the journey to his own enlightenment.

Through *Right Concentration* the monk had attained a state of mind in which fear could not enter. His spiritual practice had delivered him to a place beyond illusion and beyond its power. Unafraid of death, he lived in a fearless place. And this gave him power over worldly forces. His enlightened state did not weaken him in the world; it strengthened him.

This story is an example of the benefits of spiritual practice to the sorrowful mind; it changes our brain circuitry in relation to that which makes us suffer. It brings the mortal world into harmony with a greater truth when we see situations not through prescribed mental filters, but as they truly are. The monk, as it turned out, was more powerful than the warlord. This means that each of us, when in our right minds, is more powerful than the ego—and thus more powerful than our sadness and more powerful than our fear.

Right Concentration reminds us that simply trying to think positive thoughts is not enough to override our mental anguish. It takes the discipline of serious meditation to hone our attitudinal muscles. A vague and gauzy spirituality cannot succeed at this, but the serious practice of cultivating a thought system based on love and compassion cannot fail. Whether our meditation practice is Buddhism, Transcendental Meditation, the Workbook of *A Course in Miracles,* or any other, there is no more powerful tool for concentrating the mind on what is real.

———

Buddhism is a unique and precious gift to the planet, one embraced by many billions of people over thousands of years. As one's primary spiritual practice or as an adjunct to another, the teachings of Buddha are as deep as the deepest ocean and as wide as the heart can expand. Buddha's enlightenment furthered the spiritual evolution of humanity, and his teachings deepen our understanding—as well as our practice—of any system of spiritual truth. The Four Noble Truths and the Eightfold Path are powerful directives for how to transcend the sorrowful mind. Buddha's is a light that has illumined, and continues to illumine, a billion darkened nights.

TEN

The Light
of Moses

Generation after generation, Jews gather every year at Passover to read the story of the Exodus, the journey of the Israelites from slavery to the Promised Land. The Exodus story never changes, but with each year we do. Great religious tales are reminders of things that do not change, that we might navigate more wisely those things that do.

Judaism is both intellectually sophisticated and emotionally profound. Like Islam, the theology of the religion is deeply entwined with the history of a people. Also like other religions, it prescribes not only a way of living in the world, but also a way of surviving its ravages. The Jewish people are not unfamiliar with suffering, or with hate or prejudice or oppression. Nor is their experience of suffering in a different corner from their relationship to God. The drama of the Jews cannot be understood outside the drama of a historical pattern of rejection, but it also cannot be understood outside God's eternal promise to rescue and to deliver. The Jews take the hit—the historical pattern is obvious. But God has always delivered on His promise, and the Jews have developed a relationship with God that delivers not only Jewry but all the world to a space of possibility the ego can only temporarily disrupt. The greatest triumph of the Jews is that they have survived. In doing so, they have established a pattern of psychic survival—and triumph—that is a gift to all the world.

Every year at Passover, Jews retell the story of the Israelites being led out of slavery in Egypt, their wandering through the desert for forty years, and their ultimate deliverance to the Promised Land.

Their Exodus was led by Moses, one of the great figures of religious literature (whether or not he actually existed as one historical personage is a controversy that's fascinating but ultimately irrelevant). All the great Abrahamic religions—Judaism, Islam, and Christianity— see in Moses a global and historic messenger to the ages.

At the time of Moses's birth, the Jewish people were slaves in Egypt. According to one tradition, Egyptian astrologers told Pharaoh that on a particular day the liberator of the children of Israel was to be born, although they couldn't specify whether this liberator would be Jewish or Egyptian. To guard against any possibility that such a liberator would appear, Pharaoh decreed that all male children born that day would be drowned in the Nile.

And on that day Moses was born. Upon his entrance into the world, the house he was born in became radiant with light. Light would be a theme throughout his life—from the light that filled the house of his birth, to the burning bush out of which God spoke to him of the greatness of his mission, to the light that illumined his face when he returned from receiving the Terms of the Covenant, or the Ten Commandments, on Mount Sinai. That light—the symbol of spiritual understanding—is the light that fills any mind, or any environment, in which the thoughts of God are present. Moses, like all of us, was both informed by the light and protected by the light. Only light has the power to cast out the darkness of the ego mind. Only spiritual understanding can save us from all the insanity raging within and among us.

Moses's mother Jochebed realized that she wouldn't be able to hide Moses from the Egyptian soldiers. Heartbroken but desperate to save him, she made a waterproof basket, placed him in it, and set it down among the papyrus reeds growing on the bank of the Nile.

There is no greater pain than the pain of a mother separated from her child, and all of us have felt some aspect of violent separation from our own creations. Who among us has not felt the pain of being separated from our innocence, our happiness, our potential, our due? And have we not bravely done all we could to protect such things, to hide them away, to put them in a safe place?

Moses had a destiny greater than the forces that would defeat him, as do we all. And events unfolded in a way that provided for his survival. Pharaoh's daughter, herself having rebelled against the cruelty of the royal decree of infanticide, found the baby Moses among the reeds at the side of the Nile and raised him in the palace as her own. Significantly, it was the love of Moses's mother, her courage and her commitment to doing whatever she needed to do to protect and save him, that paved the way for his safe passage. That is a message to all of us. We may be heartbroken, but it is programmed into the nature of the universe that whenever the ego has hurt us or whatever it would take from us, the story isn't over; it has just begun. Do the loving thing, and love will find a way.

Ego is always on the lookout for ways to destroy; but spirit is always on the lookout for ways to save. The universe seeks out people and situations that are open to receiving and furthering the next formation of love. Pharaoh's daughter, having found the baby Moses among the reeds at the side of the Nile, then raised him in the palace as her own. Unbeknownst to anyone in the palace, Jochebed became Pharaoh's maid and helped raise the child. Love never dies; it simply morphs.

Notice that the cruelty in this story was demonstrated by the most powerful figure—Pharaoh. But the otherworldly forces that overcame his cruelty were channeled through the most powerless. Moses's mother had no power before Pharaoh's decree, and yet her love created a path by which Pharaoh's cruelty was undermined. Love led her to do *something*, which led to someone powerful enough within the worldly system who could take it from there.

How often it is that we might not know what to do, who to call, where to seek help, or how to find the solution to a problem when forces much greater than us are stopping us. Yet, in keeping our hearts open—in cleaving to faith and not succumbing to despair—we will do something that leads us to someone who can give us a helping hand. If Jochebed had merely given up, Moses would not have survived. Her message to the sufferer is clear: *do what you can*. When we truly embrace the realization that God has an answer to every problem, that the universe is wired for our deliverance, then we can trust that as long as we persevere, a way out of darkness will appear.

THE BURNING BUSH

Moses grew up in Pharaoh's palace, with the opportunity to escape the cruel fate of the Jewish slaves. Yet he had an emotional connection to his people; although he was not raised among the Jews, their suffering moved him. So much so, in fact, that he killed an Egyptian slave driver whom he saw beating a Jewish slave. Running away to escape retribution for his deed, he traveled to the land of Midian, began a new life as a shepherd, married, and had a child. It was there, grazing sheep one day, that he encountered the burning bush.

It's so interesting, isn't it, that Moses was a murderer? While it could be argued that his killing the slave driver was justified—maybe he would have killed the slave and Moses felt that he had no choice—it's an important reminder that the child of destiny, and that means all of us, is not without his own dark shadows. Many times we are depressed not because of what someone else did to us, but because of something that we ourselves did. And the ego, which led us to make the mistake to begin with, tells us that having made it, we are damaged goods, failures, ugly, repugnant even to God. Yet it was after Moses had committed murder that God appeared to him in the burning bush.

In other words, nothing—absolutely nothing—can make us less loved by God, less chosen by God, or less programmed by God for a destiny of greatness. If anything, our exposure to the darkness of the world, both in ourselves and in others, increases our depth of understanding, which then increases our value as conduits of His power. What the ego darkens, God illumines.

There is a beauty in the innocence of those who haven't seen enough of the world to know anything but light. There's an even greater beauty in the innocence of those who have seen so much of the world that they have seen darkness, yet then chosen light. Even when we feel we have turned our backs on God, it's important to remember that He hasn't turned His back on us. He cannot, for love is incapable of turning its back on its creations. The point is for us to choose love today, even if we didn't choose it yesterday. God didn't look at Moses and say, "What?! You expect me to *use* you after the mistakes you made?" Rather, it wasn't long after Moses made a huge mistake that God called him to greatness.

Grazing his father-in-law's flocks one day, Moses saw an angel appearing in a bush that was burning but not consumed by the fire. Angels, as defined in *A Course in Miracles,* are "thoughts of God." So Moses in a way was no different from anyone else taking a walk through nature, or "tending the flocks" by helping people in some capacity or another and having an epiphany. An awakening. A burst of enlightened understanding. A sense of knowing. This is not a different kind of inner knowing than what you or I or anyone else might have. God speaking to Moses was not an event that is different from the way He speaks to any of us; it's a symbol for the way He speaks to all of us.

And what did Moses hear from God? First, he was told to take off his sandals. The sandals are a symbol for that which touches the earth. We are told to approach God without our sandals, for the space wherein God dwells is holy ground. We surrender our worldly concerns there and come to Him with nothing but our open hearts.

We are constantly distracted today by ultimately meaningless things, all of them binding us to the regions of the earth. A twenty-four-hour news cycle, outrageous politics and world events, ridiculous gossip—all clutter our consciousness and keep us bound to the world of suffering. In approaching God, we must take off our sandals. We must "clear our heads."

In the Russian Orthodox Church, Moses's encounter with the burning bush is described as his ability to see "uncreated energies" or "glory." It is interesting that the bush was not consumed by the fire but burned continuously. God speaking to Moses from the burning bush does not signify one event, but rather a realm of consciousness that Moses visited. It is an eternal stream of divine fire burning within all hearts at all times.

Born in light (a creation of God) to a people persecuted by Pharaoh (the ego) and destined, after great trial, to be a leader (the story of the Exodus), Moses reflects the psychic journey of every soul. Each of us is born of God, then wanders into the slavery of ego consciousness, and is ultimately guided by the voice of God to travel to the promised land and take our brothers and sisters with us.

I AM WHO I AM

In his encounter with the burning bush, Moses heard the voice of God. If someone walks into a room these days and says, "God told me this" or "God told me that," we might have reason to wonder whether or not they're in touch with reality. On the other hand, if someone meditates and prays on a regular basis, then absolutely they begin to hear what in *A Course in Miracles* is called the "Voice for God." Serious spiritual practice makes you a finely tuned intuitional instrument. Just as we hear the ego's voice constantly lambasting us with negative messages, we can quiet the mind and hear the small still voice within, which is the voice for God. It's not that one sounds like Tony Bennett and the other sounds like Lady Gaga. They both sound like you. One sounds like you when you're hysterical, angry, and selfish; and the other sounds like you when you're peaceful, calm, and loving. All of us hear the voices of either ego or spirit in our heads all the time, but only one of them is the real you.

Moses knew he was hearing the voice of God, but he didn't know how he would say that to others. "Tell them," said God, "that I AM WHO I AM." This passage has been translated and interpreted in myriad ways, as are all religious stories. One interpretation says God described Himself not as "I AM WHO I AM" but rather "I AM WHO I SHALL BE." From a spiritual perspective, both are accurate—because who we are in essence exists beyond time. What's most important is the revelation that the God within us is our essential self; the essence of God is the essence of each of us, and the essence of each of us is the essence of God. When we are speaking from our true selves, or from love, we are expressing what the Voice for God has told us. Through prayer and meditation, we begin to hear the small, still Voice for God. Our purpose on earth is to then reflect, in words but also in actions, what we have heard.

The voice of God directed Moses to go back to his people, to tell them that God had chosen him to lead them out of slavery to the Promised Land.

So imagine this: You're taking a walk, and all of a sudden you have an epiphany, a sense of divine presence. And it doesn't last just for a moment; it's a high that lasts for a while. And it's not just pleasurable, it's directive. You get a feeling, a sense of mission, a calling—you have a very strong sense that God has work for you to do. You're here to help lead your people out of suffering and to peace.

What?!

And Moses has the same reaction any of us would have, basically saying, *"No way!"*

"Who am I," Moses asked God, "that I should go unto Pharaoh, and that I should bring forth the children of Israel out of Egypt?" God responded with three points: first, He rebuked Moses for having the audacity to doubt God's choice of vessel; second, He told Moses he would be aided by the wondrous powers of his staff, or rod; and third, He told Moses He would send his brother Aaron to be Moses's mouthpiece.

In other words, no matter what problems we might throw up to God as reasons for why "I can't possibly do that, Sir," his response to any argument we make is: "Actually, yes you can."

The soul is programmed for greatness of mission. When we are dissociated from that ray of light, we descend into darkness. Much unhappiness in this world is due to the fact that people are failing to perform the greatness of their missions, and they know it. Each of us has such a mission, for each of us is a child of God. Yet in failing to ask God what that mission is, and in failing to make ourselves available to Him so He might guide us to do it, we fall into the neurotic patterns of a soul that does not recognize itself or remember why it's here.

In my book *A Return to Love*, there's a paragraph that begins, "Our deepest fear is not that we are inadequate. Our deepest fear is that we are powerful beyond measure." That one paragraph, often misattributed to Nelson Mandela, has become very well known. And why? Because it points to the ego's resistance—as well as the soul's mission—to fully claiming the greatness of our potential as children of God.

The power of Moses's staff has great significance, as it refers to the power of spiritual consciousness. Like Merlin's wand, the staff is a symbol for focused, light-filled, disciplined thinking. It channels the power of thought when it travels straight down from the divine, making the human mind a conduit not only for God's *thinking* to be done on earth, but for his *will* to be done on earth.

In order to prove his power, God told Moses to throw the staff onto the ground, at which point it turned into a serpent. Moses fled in fear, but God told him to pick up the serpent by its tail—and it turned back into a staff.

The transition of the staff from terrifying serpent to miracle-making source of power refers to the relationship each of us has to the power of our own minds. The ego shrinks from spirituality because it shrinks from our greatness. It suggests that surrender to God is dangerous, that if we go there, we'll be out of control. Yet once we pick up the serpent, and take charge of our minds, then the energy of the wily serpent turns into our greatest support in performing our God-given missions.

Each of us has a staff—the unlimited power of thought—and like Moses, we are meant to use it to perform God's miracles. When our thoughts are high and loving, loving effects result; when our thoughts are low and fear-based, they do not. When Moses held up his staff, the Israelites were victorious; when he let down his staff, Israel's enemies prevailed. For him, as for us, it was not always easy to carry the staff of God. At one point Moses's hand grew tired and he didn't feel he could hold up his staff any longer. Aaron and Hur then helped support him so that "his hands remained steady until sunset." Our staffs often feel heavy and burdensome as we reach for our higher selves; such effort goes against our ego instincts. Sometimes we cannot take the high road in life without the support of friends and loved ones. But just as support arrived to hold up Moses, it arrives to hold us up as well.

MOSES'S GREAT MISSION

The story of Moses involves not only God's calling him to a great mission, but also God's helping him to perform it. *A Course in Miracles* asks whether it is reasonable to assume that God would give us a job to do and not provide us with the means to accomplish it.

God told Moses what to do and how to do it in order to free the Israelites from slavery and lead them to the Promised Land, or the "land of milk (sustenance) and honey (sweetness)." The first order of business was persuading Pharaoh to release his slaves. And are not sustenance and sweetness the main elements in happiness? Of course, Pharaoh initially refused Moses's injunction to "Let my people go."

To that, God responded with the Ten Plagues of Egypt—from

the water of the Nile turning into blood, to the land and people being covered with frogs, to lice infecting people and animals, plus seven more all the way up to and including the death of all firstborn Egyptian children—to finally convince Pharaoh that indeed he should do as God was asking. The Ten Plagues are powerful symbols of how a life lived in slavery to the ego's dictates stops *working*. First you lose your self-respect. Then you lose your friends. Then you lose your money. Then you lose your lover. At a certain point, you get the message.

The tenth plague—that is, the death of all Egyptian firstborn children—was particularly horrendous. Moses told the Israelites to put the blood of a spring lamb on the doorposts of their dwellings so that the angel of the Lord would "pass over" that house and spare the firstborn (hence the Jewish holiday of Passover). The blood of the spring lamb means the energy of the new, the innocent; it is that to which we are to devote our dwellings, or our internal selves. Metaphysically, this story is not about the children of the Egyptians being killed by God's decree; rather, it refers to the fact that wicked thoughts shall come to naught, and innocent thoughts shall be protected and blessed. In *A Course in Miracles* it says there is a limit in which we cannot miscreate.

One would think that with all Moses had done for the Israelites, they would be heartened by his appearance among them. But they were ambivalent about their journey out of Egypt; they were skeptical and resentful as much as filled with gratitude and praise. They had become accustomed to slavery; they had resigned themselves to a certain level of suffering. How often we, too, when faced with the task of making a break for freedom, see slavery to the familiarity of the ego as preferable to the uncertainty of change. Our dysfunctions can form a perverse kind of comfort zone.

We often see the voice that draws us out of bondage (the name of Moses means to "draw out") at least at first, as more a reminder of our pain than a deliverer from it. As slaves, the Israelites knew they would be fed and housed; if they fled, how could they be certain that they would survive their journey to the Promised Land? How often we too prefer the trials and tribulations of the ego to the trials and tribulations of self-actualization. We prefer to cope with our internal slavery rather than to rock the boat and make a break for freedom. We accept the false comforts of victimhood rather than assume the responsibilities of victory. Yet Moses represents the voice in all of us, always drawing us out, drawing us up, drawing us forward to the truth of who we are and the greatness of our purpose here.

EVEN IF IT TAKES A MIRACLE

Finally Pharaoh freed his slaves. And on that night, in the rush of "Hurry before he changes his mind," the Israelites fled. But when they reached the northern tip of the Red Sea, the Israelites looked back in horror to see the Egyptian army rushing toward them. Pharaoh had decided that he wanted his slaves back. The ego never retreats; it never says, "Okay, go," and actually means it. Whenever it says, "You can go now," it in fact means, "Go—until I've figured out how to get you back." It takes a miracle, a spiritual awakening, to free ourselves from the ego's clutches.

How many times have we felt despair akin to what the Israelites must have felt when they saw Pharaoh's army? They could move forward into the sea and drown, or stay in place and be overtaken by the army and killed, or returned to slavery. How often we too feel like we made a break for freedom, and are then drawn back into the ego's bondage. We need more than self-will to save us then; we need a miracle. The Israelites looked to Moses to save them, and he did.

At that moment one of the great miracles of history occurred, one of the most powerful demonstrations of God's action on behalf of His people. In that moment, God instructed Moses to raise his staff and stretch out his hand: "And Moses stretched out his hand over the sea; and the Lord caused the sea to go back by a strong east wind all that night, and made the sea dry land, and the waters were divided. And the children of Israel went into the midst of the sea upon the dry ground." Of course the Egyptian army followed, and we all know what happened to them.

The parting of the Red Sea is one of the great biblical demonstrations that God will do whatever it takes, including transcending time and space, to pave the way for His children's deliverance. The universe is programmed to rescue us from the ego's armies, whether they be our own obsessive thoughts or conditions of the outer world. We are safe to dive into the waters of spirit, even when we fear we will drown there, for God will prepare for us a safe crossing and the ego will be stilled.

Knowing that God can and will do *anything* to save His people—and all of us are His people—is one of the bulwarks of an enlightened life. A thought such as "That couldn't possibly happen" becomes replaced by, "I don't need to know *how* it will happen; I only need to know that it will." According to *A Course in Miracles,* "There's no order of difficulty in miracles."

After the Israelites crossed the Red Sea, they sang a song of celebration. Miriam the prophetess, a woman who thus spoke for God, sang, "Sing ye to the Lord, for He hath triumphed gloriously; the horse and his rider hath he thrown into the sea." This singing means the singing of our souls after we've been released from our suffering. "Singing to the Lord" is a reference to finally feeling free to express ourselves fully, without fear—to finding our own voice, our own life force, our own emotional freedom after suffering imprisonment to the ego's demands. Many of us have found ourselves "singing to the Lord" in ways we had never sung before, emerging from traumatic periods in our lives with talents and abilities that we didn't know we had before our "time in the desert," the times of our own personal despair.

THE TEN COMMANDMENTS

The crossing of the Red Sea was near the beginning of the Exodus, which lasted another forty years. In the third month after the people of Israel left Egypt, they came to the Sinai Desert. There, God called Moses up to the mountain, an event accompanied by smoke, earthquakes, and the blasting of a trumpet. For forty days and forty nights he neither ate nor drank as he received the Terms of the Covenant, known as the Ten Commandments, to be given to the nation of Israel on "two tablets of stone written with the finger of God." Living according to these tenets, the Jews were to adhere to God's law and become deliverers of His law. God told Moses to say to the people of Israel: "You have seen what I did to the Egyptians, and how I carried you on eagles' wings and brought you to Myself. Now then, if you will obey My voice and keep My agreement, you will belong to Me from among all nations. For all the earth is Mine. You will be to Me a nation of priests, a holy nation."

Just as Moses had been drawn up from the reeds at the side of the Nile and the Israelites had been drawn out of Egypt, the Ten Commandments drew from the Mind of God the prescription, the law, for right living as free men and women. Once they were no longer slaves, the Israelites were free to live as they chose. Then, even while we are living in freedom, our adherence to internal laws keeps us on the path of righteousness, the path of holiness, and the path of love.

The Terms of the Covenant reveal the principles that align us with our higher selves by aligning us with God. "Thou shalt not" in the Ten Commandments is a description of how we will behave when we are aligned with our true selves. Ultimately, "following God's laws" and "truly being ourselves" are the same thing. When Moses came down from the mountain after having received the Ten Commandments, his face shone, for he had seen God.

Although the Ten Commandments were originally handed down thousands of years ago, they have as much contemporary significance today as they ever did. For they speak to the deeper, timeless reality of what is true within us all. God's voice is ancient, and God's voice is now.

1. I am the Lord your God. You shall have no other gods before me.

Whenever you think it's the money that's going to save you, or the new job, or the prestige, or the relationship, remember that it was God who brought everything good into your life—"who brought you out of the land of Egypt, out of the house of bondage"—not the money or the job or the fame or the sex. Those things weren't there to rearrange the universe for you when you were on your knees and unable to even function; God was.

2. You shall not make for yourself a carved image . . . ; you shall not bow down to them nor serve them.

All those worldly things that you think are going to save you, that you bow down to, that you think you need to suck up to in order to have the life you want? You might want to rethink that. It's called idolatry, and it will not work. Idols will fall. Why? Because they're not God; you just sometimes get confused and think they are.

3. You shall not take the name of the Lord your God in vain.

You may think language doesn't matter, but it does. Words have power. Being careless with your words is as destructive as being careful with them is creative. This world is not a joke, and neither is the divine within you. Talking about God in a trashy way is talking about yourself in a trashy way. Don't expect anything good to come from that.

4. Remember the Sabbath day and keep it holy.

Your nervous system can only take so much. You're not a human do-ing; you're a human being. All this rush rush rush, work work work, gotta go gotta go is destroying your adrenal glands, leaching the juice out of your life force, and making you make dumb decisions that affect your life and the lives of others. One day a week. Just one day. Make your "Sabbath" about important things, deep things, loving things. Regroup, turn within, and recalibrate your energies to align with God. The other six days, a bit of time each day is good. But on the Sabbath, give God the whole thing. You'll live longer, be healthier, and be happier if you do.

5. Honor your father and your mother.

You probably don't need the Ten Commandments to tell you there's no way to be happy without figuring out your childhood drama and getting straight with your parents. If they were good, they probably deserve more kindness and respect than you're giving them now. And if they weren't so good, you're still going to have to forgive them, or else your relationships will be messed up throughout your life.

6. You shall not murder.

Hard to believe you still need to hear this one, but you're still killing, spending huge material resources on building more killing machines, and basically ignoring this commandment. The ego is big on "strong defense" and the Second Amendment. But, then, the ego is a killer . . .

7. You shall not commit adultery.

It's time to admit that over-casualizing sex is harmful to yourself and to others. Sex is one of the most powerful forces in the universe, one that can heal and one that can harm. You go messing around with that energy, someone some-where is bound to get hurt. And it might be you. If sex doesn't stem from a sacred commitment, then it doesn't stem from God. Whether the commitment was yours or someone else's, it is yours to honor.

8. You shall not steal.

   Once again, it's amazing that you still need to be reminded about this. But corporations are still stealing seeds, nations and corporations are still stealing territory, and the rich are still stealing from the poor. And we put up with this!

9. You shall not bear false witness against your neighbor.

   Once again, words have power. Negative gossip, slander, hate speech—these things can destroy people's careers, even their lives. It doesn't matter whether someone was in the room when you made unkind or unfair remarks; think of the universe as having ears. Words are energy, and energy takes form. Whatever you say will boomerang back in your direction.

10. You shall not covet.

    God made an infinitely abundant universe. Your neighbor having something great doesn't diminish your ability to have it, too. But if you withhold your blessing from their success, it will only limit your ability to attract the same. You only get to have in life what you're willing to bless in the lives of others.

RESPONDING TO THE CALL

As they wandered through the desert, the journey of the Israelites continued to be difficult and continued to involve miracles. God rained mana from heaven, and covered their camp with quail for the hungry wanderers to eat. God gave Moses the power in his hands to hold back an army who was trying to defeat them. The bond between God and the Israelites grew deeper during this time of their suffering. At one point, God commanded Moses to strike a rock with his staff when the Israelites needed water to drink. Not seeing water immediately, Moses struck the rock a second time. For this, God punished Moses by denying him entrance into the Promised Land. What this means, metaphysically, is that lack of faith diminishes our power and denies us inner peace. The problem for many of us, much of the time, is not that we don't hear what God is saying; it's that we don't *believe* what God is saying, or we don't *like* what God is saying. Then, putting our faithlessness into action, we do or say something that actually interrupts His plan and deflects our miracle. But life will continue to "draw us" to our destiny of deeper relationship with God and more powerful performance of the tasks to which he assigns us.

All of us make an Exodus in our lives; all of us are delivered from slavery to the Promised Land by a mysterious hand. The Exodus is our journey through suffering, as we suffer from bondage at the hands of the ego to freedom in the hands of God.

Moses reminds us that God is God; He led the Israelites out of slavery and beyond their suffering, and He shall do the same for us. Sometimes during the slavery years, sometimes during the desert years, and sometimes during the promised years, we are sustained by the words, "Hear, O Israel, the Lord our God, the Lord is One. Amen."

The great religious traditions provide the tales of enlightened beings to inspire us to continue on our own hero's journey, knowing that although we too fight illusions, although we too wander, and although we too suffer, we are bound for the inevitable glory that the journey ultimately leads to.

The suffering of the Jews at the hands of Pharaoh is a foundational myth in human history, imprinting upon our consciousness the relationship between the children of God and the ego that taunts us. The ego is indeed a mental slave driver. It is the unconscious part of us that leads us time and time again to self-sabotage—to undermine our relationships, resist recovery, make stupid decisions, and so forth. It is the part of us that interprets everything that happens in the most negative way possible. It is the part of us that insists that there is no hope. It represents, as well, any outer forces that would hold us down.

The ego has only one goal: your suffering; while God has another: your deliverance. Whether it's the suffering of age, disease, and death to which the Buddha bore witness; or the suffering of the Jews as slaves or as they wandered in the desert; or the suffering of Jesus on the cross—all three stories bear witness to the viciousness of the ego mind.

However much evil appears in the world, in time it is replaced by the reemergence of love. The Creator of the universe overrules the force that would obstruct His plan. The arc of the universe moves, however slowly, in the direction of good.

One of the most amazing things about great religious stories is how psychologically astute they are. Serving God—that is, extending love—is not just something we "should" do. It is the only way to be happy. But getting to that point, genuinely burning through all the shadows within ourselves so the light of our true beings can shine through, is a journey. It is a process; it is not a fact. And that process can be hard.

The forty years during which the Israelites suffered on their way to the Promised Land were not easy. Becoming genuinely self-aware, burning through the layers of the false self, can be deeply painful. Our current culture responds to this pain with promises of short-term relief. But some of the times we spend in the desert turn out to be groundwork for our own re-greening. There, in the desert, many of us see our first miracles.

The great religious stories are not simply stories but coded messages from God to all of us. God dwells in the quantum field of no-time, no-space, and what he conveyed to anyone He is conveying to everyone. He will lead *us* out of slavery, and He will lead *us* to enlightenment's door. What greater blessing could we receive than God telling us that He will deliver us "to Myself"?

In being delivered to God, we're delivered from the illusion of who we are to the reality of who we truly are. We go from being addicted to being sober; from being needy to being independent; from being afraid to being brave. We're dying to the parts of ourselves that need to die in order to give birth to what is trying to be born. We're burning through a lot of ego on our way to the life that lies beyond it, having to face whatever we need to face before we can face God. And this is painful, perhaps even torturous. It is humiliating. It is terrifying. But that journey through the spiritual wilderness is not a waste, for it leads to the Promised Land at last.

THE DEATH OF MOSES

When Moses was 120 years old, he climbed Mount Nebo, and God showed him the land all the way to the Mediterranean Sea, saying: "This is the land I promised on oath to Abraham, Isaac, and Jacob when I said, 'I will give it to your descendants.' I have let you see it with your eyes, but you will not cross over into it." Moses himself was not allowed to enter the Promised Land.

In this, Moses was like Susan B. Anthony, who devoted her life to women's suffrage but herself did not live to see the passage of the Nineteenth Amendment giving women the right to vote; or Martin Luther King Jr., who said he'd seen the Promised Land but added "I might not get there with you." The generation that still retains the memory of slavery is not always the one to be completely delivered from it. The story of the Jews is the story of a people, a story of generations that come and go, of efforts made by one generation then followed by efforts of the next.

Joshua, who had been born in the desert, would enter the Promised Land as leader of the Israelites. God told him: "Be strong and brave. Do not be terrified. Do not lose hope. I am the Lord your God. I will be with you everywhere you go."

Extreme suffering has marked the history of the Jewish people in modern as well as ancient times. A continuous thread of anti-Semitism and its attendant evils dates back many centuries, from pogroms in Europe and Russia to anti-Semitic incidents on the rise in many places even now. During the Holocaust—the almost unspeakable mass murder of 6 million Jews by the Nazis roughly between 1941 and 1945—some were reported to have uttered God's words to Joshua as they entered the gas chambers, "Do not be terrified. I am with you wherever you go."

The Promised Land is above all else a state of consciousness. Seeing it only in geographical terms has not worked, is not working, and will not work. It is a state of mind, an inner peace that alone will guarantee outer peace for our children and our children's children. The Covenant is not only a promise God made, but the terms of the relationship we are to have with Him. It is the light of understanding of both who we are in God and who He would have us be in the world. Having suffered, surely we are called to be exquisitely sensitive to the suffering of others; having been as oppressed as we have been, to be the most resistant to any temptation to oppress. God's call to be a holy nation, like the call to be a holy individual, is not without its pain. In the words of my father, "The lessons God throws the Jews are never, ever easy." The journey of the Israelites began thousands of years ago and continues to this day—as fraught as ever, as dramatic as ever, and as powerful as ever. God is with us still, and will be with us wherever we go.

ELEVEN

The Light of Jesus

The life of Jesus was a historical fact, to be sure; but it is also a mystical one. He is a timeless conduit of spiritual force—not just one man who lived two thousand years ago, but also a psychic reality that all of us are experiencing all the time. His birth represents our own rebirth; his ministry represents our own path to follow; and his death and resurrection represent our own capacity to transcend pain, sorrow, and death.

Buddha's observation of suffering led to his search for enlightenment; Moses's compassion for the suffering of his people enabled him to hear the voice of God directing him to lead them out of slavery; and Jesus's suffering on the cross condenses the sorrows and tears and pain of humanity into a single incident. Most importantly, his resurrection reflects God's response to our suffering: that in Him, all suffering ends.

The suffering of Jesus on the cross was an embodiment of the full viciousness of the ego. His crucifixion is the ultimate symbol of the ego having gotten its wish, causing us to suffer and ultimately to die. The ego is the belief that we *are* our bodies, and thus the death of the body seems to be the ego's ultimate triumph. The resurrection is God's response to the crucifixion, the reemergence of truth after illusion has had its way with us. It is the ultimate reemergence of the light after darkness. It is the fact that death does not exist, for what God created cannot die. It is the expression of God's will, which has never not been done, not only in Jesus's life, but also in ours. No matter what happens, no matter what evil might occur, God always has and always will get the ultimate final word; in time, all will be well. In fact, it will be glorious.

Because spiritual reality applies to a state of awareness beyond time and space, the acceptance of the resurrection takes us beyond mere hope. We do not just *hope* that everything will work out in time. We *know* it will work out in time because in the Mind of God it already has. In the Mind of God—the quantum field of infinite love—everything is already perfect. We can therefore proclaim our resurrection while in the midst of our crucifixion; as it says in *A Course in Miracles,* "miracles collapse time." We don't wait for circumstances to change to know that things are perfect. We accept that things are perfect, and our conviction causes circumstances to change. The power as always lies in our thinking, as we affirm that God *is.* And so it is that we make it so.

CHRISTMAS

Christmas and Easter are two existential bookends that underlie every situation. The first represents a choice, always available to us, to give birth to our better selves. The second represents the fact that no matter what tricks the ego may play, the Spirit of God will return our lives to divine perfection.

The story of Jesus began, of course, with the story of his mother. She was "awakened from her slumber"—that is, aroused from the stupor of the ego mind—and told, as all of us are, that we can be more than we think we are. God has chosen us to impregnate with his seed—His Spirit penetrates our consciousness—and as we hold it within us and allow it to grow, it will then produce new life within us. Mothered by our humanness and fathered by the Spirit of God, the Christ is then born onto the earth.

Free will determines whether the Mary inside us says, "Yes God, please use me; allow my mind, my body, my self to be the container for your Spirit and the womb through which you incarnate." Mary represents the feminine consciousness through which, should we choose, we make ourselves available to be used by God. Christ is a name for the being who then emerges when we do.

Beyond the body, beyond the material plane, on the level of spirit, we are not separate. For God created all of us as one. This is the metaphysical meaning of the statement "There is only one begotten Son." Jesus is a name for the oneness we all share. To join on the level of Christ is to simply realize that we are already one.

The Christ Mind is the mind we all share, beyond the body. In fact, we are like the spokes of a wheel. If you identify the spokes with their position on the rim, then they are many and separate. But if you identify the spokes with the point at which they originate, you see that all spokes emerge from the same point. That point of oneness, that shared source point, is called by many names—one of which is the Christ.

Michelangelo felt God had already created a great statue such as the *Pietà*, or *David*, and the sculptor's job was simply to get rid of the excess marble surrounding it. So all of us have within us the eternal self, the perfect self, the unchangeable self that is God's creation. Enlightenment means dissolving the fearful thoughts that surround and obscure it.

One name for this shared self is Jesus. He was one in whom all fear-based thought was dissolved; thus he became one with the Christ. By remembering him, we remember who we really are.

CRUCIFIXION

We come into this world as innocent beings, yearning to love and yearning to receive love, but the ego has its way with all of us. It seeks to crucify our innocence, to invalidate our love, to make us suffer, and to kill us if it can. It is the aspect of the mind that repudiates God.

The suffering of Jesus on the cross symbolizes all the suffering the ego has ever caused or ever will. One human being—suffering through the worst torture, while completely loving those who tortured him—broke the ego's sword in half. Because all minds are joined, when anyone achieves anything, their achievement becomes available for everyone. Jesus broke the ego's spell by surrendering his mind so completely to God that the spell is now broken for everyone.

The body is the level of the crucifixion; the spirit is the level of the resurrection. Jesus demonstrates the power of love to overcome our crucifixions. The spiritual lesson in any situation does not have to do with what has been done to us, but with how we interpret what has been done to us. We experience ourselves as beholden to whichever universe we choose to identify with. If I identify only with the three-dimensional universe, then the ego will have its way with me; but if I identify with the spiritual universe, the ego is powerless to affect me.

Each of us is responsible for what we choose to think. If I identify only with my body, then I'm identifying with my weakness and will interpret the world in a way that fortifies my sense of weakness; but if I identify with the Christ, I am identifying with my strength and will interpret the world in a way that fortifies my sense of strength. Whether my crucifixion is in the area of health, relationships, money and career, or anything else does not matter. The crucifixion takes many different forms but the resurrection is formless. There is only one real problem and one real answer. God's Answer is the same no matter the particularity of the problem. In any situation, as I remove my barriers to love I invoke the miraculous power of God to transform it. Crucifixion is the energy pattern by which the ego seeks to ruin our lives. Resurrection is the return to love and thus the over-riding of ego.

That is why love is always the answer. It doesn't necessarily *feel* that in any situation the question "Who do I need to forgive?" is relevant to the exercise of my power and the return of deep sanity. But it is. Only when I am in a state of pure love am I in my power, for only that is the power of God. And from that, all miracles follow.

RESURRECTION

The resurrection is not just an article of faith but an existential fact. It is simply a description of how the universe operates—life always reasserting itself even when the forces of death and darkness have temporarily prevailed. It is an otherworldly event that recreates the world. Like a tiny flower growing through cracks in broken cement, peace of mind emerges at last after periods of grief have ravaged the heart. Time and time again, love reappears after even the most crushing events. And though in time our bodies are finally let go, in fact there is no time, and in God there is no death.

Jesus said, "Take heart, for I have overcome the world." He did not say, "Don't worry; I've fixed everything." To fix and to overcome are two distinctly different things. To fix is to change things on the worldly plane; to overcome is to evolve beyond the consciousness of this world entirely.

To some, Jesus is a teacher; to some, he is a transmission. He is either or both in our lives, whichever we choose. The genuine spiritual experience is one in which we move beyond mere intellectual understanding to a visceral change within us.

Some ask, "But you don't believe the resurrection actually occurred physically! You do think it's just a *metaphor*, right?" But such argument is facile. The resurrection is a psychic reality, whether it occurred physically or not. It is more than a symbol. It is a spiritual imprint of infinite possibility, accomplished by one and now available to all.

Faith in the resurrection is simply a recognition of how the universe operates. For miracles, being of God, are natural. There are objective, discernible laws of the internal universe, just as there are objective, discernible laws of the external universe. Just as physical gravity weighs things down, love is a spiritual antigravitational force ensuring that whatever goes down will ultimately rise back up. Ego pulls all things down, and then—wherever love is present—they are lifted back up again. But we must align our minds with love in order for the principle to appear operative in our lives.

If we choose to believe this truth cannot be true, then it still remains true but we are blinded to it. Miracles are always available, but if our inner eye is closed then we cannot see. Opportunities appear and we do not recognize them; help arrives but we don't appreciate it so we fail to take advantage of the miracle it offers; love stands in front of us but we let it slip away. *A Course in Miracles* says we're like people in a very bright room, holding our fingers in front of our eyes and complaining that it is dark in here.

Jesus's complete surrender to God—or correction of perception—made him one with the Atonement. According to *A Course in Miracles*, he has been authorized by God to be an Elder Brother to those who call on him for help as we journey on the path of our own enlightenment. In remembering him, we remember God. In remembering his power, we remember our own. His mind, when joined with our mind, shines away the ego. Any condition of crucifixion in our lives is then miraculously transformed.

But it takes three days, of course.

And what does this mean? It means that as we change our thinking during the time of deepest darkness, we initiate the process by which light will reassert itself. It takes time within the linear plane—this period symbolized by the forty years the Israelites spent in the desert and the three days between the crucifixion and resurrection—for worldly conditions to catch up with our change in consciousness. Spirit having readjusted our thinking on the level of cause, effects then automatically change. While living in the world, we think thoughts that are not of this world, which gives us mastery within it.

When we keep our hearts open even when they're breaking, when we seek to love others even when they have denied us their love, we are thinking like Jesus and share his resurrection. Jesus will—if we request it—lend us his power, join his mind with ours to shine away the ego, stand in the breach between our ego and spirit, and thus save us from the insanity of the ego mind. That is what it means to say Jesus casts out demons: when our minds are surrendered to his care, we are lifted beyond our neuroses and pathologies and fear.

How does he heal the sick and raise the dead? When the leper stood before Jesus, he stood before someone whose mind had been healed of worldly illusion. Jesus saw not only with the physical eye but with the inner eye, the spiritual eye, the vision of the Holy Spirit. When he looked at the leper, he saw through the illusion of a sick body to the perfect being, the Christ, within the man. As with Moses, Jesus's alignment with the Mind of God bestowed upon him the power to lift all things to divine right order. In *A Course in Miracles* it says that miracles arise from conviction. Jesus simply didn't believe in leprosy, because he knew that only love is real. His mind so convinced, in his presence the leper could not believe in it either—and so the leper was healed.

That's what it means to be a miracle-worker: to be the presence of the Alternative, one whose mind has been so healed of the illusions of the world that in our presence, illusions are dissolved. We look to the great spiritual masters of the world who have accomplished this, those such as Jesus, as elder brothers and sisters, as teachers, as beacons of what is possible for us.

In *A Course in Miracles* it is said that Jesus didn't have anything we don't have, that he simply didn't have anything else. That he dwelled in a state that is potential within us all. That as we ask him to enter our minds, he will help to guide us to that state too. The crucifixion is a personal event, a human story; but the resurrection is a spiritual fact, a collective field of infinite possibility that all of us share. We can spiritually leapfrog over the regions of suffering and experience the glory of suffering's end.

Both crucifixion and resurrection are extraordinary powers at work in our lives, just as they were in the life of Jesus. They are psychic realities, the understanding of which adds depth to the understanding of our own lives. With this understanding, we gain the ability to more wisely navigate our experience of the world. To not feel our suffering is to deny the crucifixion; but to not let go of it is to deny the resurrection. Though we might have fallen, we will yet rise.

EASTER

Easter is the symbol of the resurrection, the crowning accomplishment of the forgiving mind. It represents the triumph of love and the healing potential within every moment. It represents a reason to hope when all hope seems lost, the potential for light that exists within even the deepest darkness, and the possibility for new beginnings that seem impossible when all has gone wrong.

As a principle, resurrection does not require our recognition in order to exist. But as a practical reality, it requires our willingness in order to manifest. Our openness to infinite possibility—the willingness to consider that there might be another way, that a miracle might be possible—makes us available to miracles. We become pregnant with possibilities, once having allowed the thought of infinite possibility to penetrate our consciousness.

Where parts of us have died—to hope, to growth, to creativity—God restores our crucified selves to new life, restoring the cosmic order to situations in which even the most horrifying chaos reigned before.

Human suffering is inevitable in a world that is permeated with illusion and fear, yet through the power of forgiveness we can and do transform it. With every prayer, every moment of faith, every act of mercy, every instant of contrition, every effort at forgiveness, in time we move beyond our suffering. We die to who we used to be and are reborn as who we are meant to be, thus lifted above darkness and ignorance and death.

Each of us goes through this—we all have our own crucifixions, our own battles and trials and tribulations. But each of us has within us as well the potential for resurrection, as an indwelling God both calls us out of darkness and delivers us to light. Resurrection, salvation, and enlightenment are the same.

Three days after Jesus was crucified, the women who were closest to him went to the tomb to claim his body, but they did not find it. Suddenly two angels appeared and said to them: "Why do you look for the living among the dead? He isn't here, but has been raised" (Luke 24:5–6).

What does this mean, metaphysically? It means that once we have survived a personal crisis and been delivered to a higher level of understanding, the part of our personality that was crucified by the event no longer exists. God nullifies the effects of that which made us cry. We don't just "work through" our issues; we are "saved" from them.

The angels' announcement that Christ's dead body does not exist, that the crucified Christ has risen, means that the aspect of yourself that self-sabotaged, or was victim to someone else's sabotage, need no longer appear within your personality. Your neurotic patterns, your bitterness and hopelessness; such aspects of self, when healed by God, are transmuted into who you are now. You are no longer stuck in fear, no longer blinded by ego, and no longer nailed to the cross of your own crucifixion. "Hallelujah!" seems too small a word.

Understanding anew, we become new. We are not just improved; we are *changed*. This process is both an awakening and a journey, as we emerge from the torment of facing our own demons into the light of having faced them down.

The benefits of the journey are cumulative. We become different because of what we've been through. We become wiser, nobler, more humble, and more aware. We become more peaceful and more open to the miracles of life. The holiest work of all is finding this wholeness within, where all the broken pieces of our selves have converged in forgiveness and love. Such is the miracle of redemption: transformation and personal rebirth.

JESUS AS SAVIOR

Having been "saved" from ego consciousness, Jesus now has the role of savior to those of us still lost within it. He is someone who, having risen above illusions in his own mind, has been authorized by God to help anyone who calls to him to do the same. The ego's exclusive, fear-based interpretation of the story of Jesus has been one of the great tragic ironies of the world. As it says in *A Course in Miracles,* "some bitter idols have been made of him who came only to be brother to the world." We testify to the power of Jesus in our lives by demonstrating his love, and we testify to his resurrection by living it.

To follow Jesus means to *love as he loved,* for unconditional love is our one and only salvation. To teach is to demonstrate. Jesus does not ask us to be martyrs for him, but teachers—people who demonstrate the healing that occurs when our minds are made whole in God. When he said to his disciples, "Go into the countryside and teach my gospel," he did not mean, "Go out into the world and hit people over the head with our book." He meant, "Go out into the world and *be love.*" That is the same thing as enjoining us to go out into the world and work miracles, for as we think with love, miracles occur naturally. Anyone who loves the world is a savior of the world.

All genuine spiritual paths are paths of spiritual salvation in that they're a healing of the mind. Salvation is when we learn to think as God thinks. Having actualized the consciousness of the divine that is potential in us all, Jesus now has the power to help *us* rise to the vibrational frequency of that consciousness, should we ask him to. When the mind is filled with light, there is no darkness. When the mind is one with Christ, the ego does not exist.

It's in vogue these days to simply say, "Just change your thoughts!" But such a change isn't always easy, and certainly not when we're in the grips of a depressing time in our lives. We can't just analyze our depression and expect it to dissolve. There are times when we need a miracle to help us rise above our tears. We need help in going from what we know abstractly to what we actually feel. Jesus is one of the powers that can deliver us from the grips of fear and into the arms of love.

THE DIVINE MIND

It was the *mind* of Buddha that awakened under the Bodhi tree. It was the *mind* of Moses that channeled God's power to part the Red Sea. And it was the *mind* of Jesus that channeled God's power. The mind when unaligned with God is the cause of all suffering; the mind when aligned with God is the cause of suffering's end.

Two men were crucified with Jesus, one to his left and one to his right. But there is no tale of *their* resurrections. Why? Because their minds, theoretically, were not illumined. Jesus did not speak of hate for his accusers, or blame those around him. He loved even those who hated him. His mind was so purely aligned with the unconditionally loving Spirit of God that all the power of God was given unto him. He is the "light of the world" because he is the light inside our minds.

Jesus is a portal, as are all great spiritual systems. They are doors to a field of inexpressible love and power. But the portal means nothing if we don't walk through it. Our aspiration as spiritual seekers is to lift our consciousness so close to God's that we become masters, not slaves, of the mortal world—just like the Buddhist monk who calmly defied the warlord, like Moses parting the Red Sea, and like Jesus rising from the dead.

To the sufferer, this is not a matter of theology or metaphysics; it is a matter of surviving an experience. Regardless of what name is on the door through which we pass on our way to God, opening the door makes all the difference. No words are more powerful than "Dear God, I choose to come into You. Please come into me. Amen."

The miracle is that God will come in, for He is already there. And when we see that, we are amazed by the light in Him and in our selves. Our amazement then turns into joy, our tears turn into triumph, and peace returns at last.

I have borne witness to much agony in my life. I have seen, and I have experienced, the pain of heartbreak. Yet in the lives of others, as in my own life as well, I have seen deep darkness turn into light. I have seen hope again in the eyes of those who formerly had none. I have glimpsed how the universe operates. I have seen the glory of God. I am a witness to resurrection. I know in my heart that it is true.

TWELVE

Tears to Triumph

No one book or healing session or religious service is going to stop all our tears. The spiritual medicine that heals our sadness is not a pill or a shot; it's an internal process of awakening from a dream that is posing as reality. Given that our entire culture is predicated on thoughts that separate us, belittle us even to ourselves, and breed fear of anyone and everything, it is no surprise so many people feel as though they live under a very dark cloud.

Your true self knows you are one with the universe, created in the perfect image of God, eternally innocent, blessed and protected, here only to love and forgive. This true self, by whatever name we call it, is obscured beneath layers of illusion. At this point your true self is so used to crouching within the cage to which the ego has assigned it, it's as though it has forgotten how to stand forth in glory. We lack the psychological skill sets that lead to joy.

We cultivate the emotional habits of sadness more than the emotional habits of happiness. We've been so trained to think thoughts of fear and attack that the mental musculature to support our joy has shriveled.

And it is up to each of us to rebuild those muscles, no different than it is up to us to strengthen the muscles of our bodies. We generally agree that we are responsible for many things about our lives, but somehow not our emotions. In fact, happiness derives from a decision we make. We might not be happy today, but as long as we've developed the musculature of happiness then we will find the internal strength to return to it.

People for the most part go through crises the way we go through life in general. If I consistently perceive myself as at the mercy of the changing tides of circumstance, projecting onto people or things that they are the source of my happiness, then I am bound to cry when the person or circumstance doesn't do as I wish. At that point, I will be tempted to hold a grievance against that person or circumstance, which will only increase my pain.

My mind, therefore, is the source of my sadness. And my mind is the source of my happiness. Only I get to choose how I use my mind, but however I choose to use it will determine whether I'm on my way to pain or on my way to peace.

One day I was in an airport gift shop browsing through fashion magazines. While I admired the beautiful pictures I also noticed that with every page, I started feeling worse about myself. My face.

My body. My age. My clothes. And then I realized I was starting to buy one of those magazines! I quickly put it down like it was a hot coal, thinking, "Why should I do that to myself?!" I was going straight from an experience that made me feel bad to an effort to get more of it. This is not to say that such magazines have no place in life, but for me on that particular day—not so much.

And do we not do that to ourselves consistently? We are so sucked into a modern brew of loveless perceptions that we are tempted to think that we have no choice. And that, right there, is where the awakening begins. We do have a choice. We always have a choice.

DECIDING TO BE HAPPY

From Buddha's Eightfold Path to the Ten Commandments to the Workbook of *A Course in Miracles,* any serious spiritual teaching involves more than a prescription for feeling good. Enlightenment is serious work.

In order to survive and thrive, humanity must disavow a fictional worldview that poses as reality. Spirituality is a radical realization that the body's senses tell us lies, that time is not what it appears to be, and that the universe is more malleable than we thought. At first all this is a terrible shock, but ultimately it becomes such a joy to know. While it rattles us at first to learn that we're not who we think we are and the world isn't what we thought it was, once it finally hits us what that means, then it's a source of complete relief.

This moment of realization, this surrender of limited perspective and openness to miracles, signifies the death of the ego. But like Pharaoh responding to Moses's demand that the Israelites be released from slavery, the ego says, "Nope. Not so fast." One moment of egolessness is not necessarily followed by a moment of more egolessness, so much as by a moment of panic. The ego puts up some strong defenses. Too much love will not be tolerated, and too much forgiveness will simply not do.

How attached we are at times to our suffering. To the ego, after all, pain is a peak experience. In certain ways, we've created a cultural propensity to what author Caroline Myss calls "woundology." We get more support in our society for the places where we are wounded than for the places where we are healed. We're more apt to find camaraderie among those who share our tears than among those who share our joy.

There is an emotional art to balancing the allowance of our suffering with the certitude that this too shall pass. And that certainty doesn't just rest on our faith in God. It must rest on our faith in ourselves. We must develop a way of talking to ourselves much like the way we talk to our children: ". . . *because I said so.*" I will survive this because I *choose* to survive this. There is a difference between a dark valley where you know God walks with you, and a hellish descent into a bottomless abyss. The bottomless abyss is not of God and if you ever find yourself falling into it, get on the case with whatever tools come into your mind. "Satan get thee behind me" works. Imagining a crucifix thrust toward a vampire works. Falling to your knees and crying "God, please help me" works.

Because you *must* get up. We need you here. Perhaps your children need you or your partner needs you. And even if neither of those exist, the world still needs you. For you, like everyone, are a precious child of God, and there would be a huge hole in the universe if you decided to check out. Perhaps you cannot see your strengths, but they are within you because God put them there. Perhaps you cannot see a future, but it exists in the Mind of God. Perhaps you cannot imagine being happy again, but you will be because God has heard your prayer and has miracles in store for you.

The ego torments you, as it torments us all. But the ego is a liar and what it says to you is not true. You are not dried up, or useless, or damaged, or a failure, or a loser, or a problem to have around. As long as you are alive, and even longer, you are of infinite value. You are God's eternally innocent creation, no matter what anyone thinks of you or what anyone has done to you, or anything you've done wrong or any failure you might have experienced. As low as you feel you might have fallen, that is how high you will rise in God. He will gently scoop you up in His hands and lift you to the highest heights.

And He will do this for His sake. Not because you're a nice person, which you may or may not be. He will do it because that is what love does, because He cannot turn His back on His children though we so consistently turn our back on Him. He will do it because His creativity and His mercy are without end. He will do it not just because He loves you, but *because He is love.*

And His love is infinite. Your cowering beneath the weight of the ego's monstrous force is not God's will for you or for anyone. Love is the victor. The battle has already been won. You do not have to fight for the victory, but simply accept it as already accomplished. For only what is love is real, no matter what shape or size or form the nightmarish hallucination might now be taking in your life.

Hold on, be strong, have faith until tomorrow comes. For no dark night has ever not been followed by the glorious radiance of God's new day. Surrender to Him and ask Him to help you. Then get up, wash your face, dry your tears, and show up to help someone else—someone who is having as hard a time, perhaps even harder, holding on today as you are. Turning your compassion to their weakness, you will find your strength.

None of us ever knows what suffering lurks beneath the brave exterior of anyone we meet. But it is reasonable to assume that no matter what suffering we have endured, whoever stands to our left and whoever stands to our right has suffered as much as we have. A deep river of agony underlies the templates of mortal consciousness, as all of us struggle mightily to survive in a world that refuses to see us, or hear us, or love us as we would wish to be seen and heard and loved.

Feeling that way does not make you odd. It makes you human. It means you feel the exquisite pain of being a stranger in a strange land, and you have made your way to the extraordinary realization that the material world is not your home. The fact that you cannot bear it here is entirely valid. The point is, understanding this is not the end. It is the beginning. You're not at home in this world, but you are at home in the arms of God.

He has sent you here to reclaim this plane of existence for the light that is at the heart of things. Earth has been held hostage for a very long time, the human race imprisoned here within our own minds, seemingly limited to the very small pieces of joy the ego will allow. But you're not here to be a prisoner in this world. You're here to help set it free.

Has not your suffering helped in some way to make you more aware of humanity's frailty? Has it not expanded your compassion for those who walk with you? Has it not in some way prepared you for a larger life?

When you remember who you really are, and the glorious purpose of your existence here, then you will fall to your knees again—this time not in pain but in gratitude, overwhelmed by the blessing and privilege of having been given such a miracle as this life you get to live. You'll ask that God make of you a shining star in the darkened skies of the world, that you might represent His love and reflect His goodness for those who cry as you have cried. Whatever problems you have, simply put them in His hands now. He will handle them for you, as He turns you into someone who can handle them yourself. You'll emerge much stronger, and be ready to work miracles in the lives of others as God worked miracles in yours.

God Himself will wipe away all tears and that will wipe away all doubt. When the morning comes, you will hardly remember the pain of this night. The memory will only appear when it is useful for you to remember, that others might be strengthened by you and you be strengthened by them. Look forward, not backward. To the light, and not to the dark. To God and not to anyone or anything less powerful or pure, for only God is God and only God can do what your ego says cannot be done: lift you up and raise you high.

The darkness has no power before the light within your heart. Be patient. Give it time, if it needs time. God will give you back not only the life you thought you lost but also one you never dreamed possible. Having suffered, you will have a taste for sweetness and a talent for happiness and an appetite for peace. You will be a bearer of sweetness and a bearer of happiness and a bearer of peace—for your sake, for God's sake, and for the sake of all the world.

Such are the rewards of holding on and trusting in the Lord. For God is good. God is great. And God is true.

Amen.

Acknowledgments

Writing a book is not easy. Part of the process is exhilarating, but part of it is not.

I was helped in very significant ways as I wrote this one, and I want to deeply thank the individuals who pored over the words, chapters, and issues I was writing about almost as much as I did. I could not have written this book without them.

Cindy DiTiberio, Liana Gergely, India Williamson, and Wendy Zahler all added immeasurably to the editing process. Each of them was there when I needed them, like angels lifting me, pushing me, even shoving me over the finish line.

My thanks to Mickey Maudlin for giving me the opportunity to write the book, and trusting that I had something of value in mind when I proposed the idea. As usual, it's an honor to work under his supervision and guidance.

Thanks to Ellis Levine for providing me excellent literary legal counsel and support; to Tammy Vogsland for holding my material world together; and to Laurie DiBenedetto, Crista Hope, Catherine

Roberts, and Tammy Brenizer for keeping the wheels turning so that I can do what I do.

Thanks as well to Katie Piel, Alex Yerik, Irene Csara, and Mike Burns for valuable assistance.

Thanks to the wonderful team at HarperOne: Lisa Zuniga, Anna Paustenbach, Melinda Mullin, Terri Leonard, Laura Lind, and Jessie Dolch, for your patience as well as excellence.

Thanks to Frances Fisher, David Kessler, Victoria Pearman, Candace Block, Alana Stewart, Stacie Maier, Alyse Martinelli, and Lane Bowes for the bonds and treasures of friendship.

Also to Ora Nadrich, Ben Decker, Jamie Adler, Katherine Woodward Thomas, Lawrence Koh, Jonathan Duga, and Tara Margolin, for gifts of kindness I will not forget.

Thank you again to my daughter, India, who is also my best friend, part-time editor, business supervisor, biggest blessing, and greatest joy. No mother was ever more proud, or more grateful, or more in love.

Thank you to the many people who were so kind to me during some changes in my own life over the past few years. The support, friendship, and generosity shown to me are gifts for which I can never fully express my gratitude. Hopefully, with this book I have expressed some lessons learned.

Thank you to everyone who has read my books, come to my events, helped at my workshops, or in any way has shared your story with me. I hold each of you in my heart, and those are not just words.